Contents

KW-552-910

c h a p t e r • 1

The world and me

This chapter will help to explore the many kinds of relationships that we have with ourselves and the world around us, by focusing on Christianity, Buddhism, Humanism, Hinduism and Sikhism.

'The unexamined life is not worth living.'
Socrates – a Greek philosopher

Are we all in the same world?

Humans can get things amazingly wrong sometimes. Imagine all those people who lived in medieval times, for example. They – like millions of people before them – were all sure that the world was flat! A terrifying Hell lay 'beneath' them, with a beautiful Heaven 'above'. The Sun was even thought to spin around the Earth right up until the sixteenth century. This was wrong, and yet it seemed true at the time. This raises a big question for us: are we really so sure that we are getting things right now?

Have you ever felt frightened, only to wake and realize that you were just having a nightmare? Or perhaps you were convinced that there was a pool of water in the distance and then realized it was only a mirage? If our feelings and eyes can fool us, what else might we be mistaken about? This unit will help you explore how we view the world around us: our relationship with our surroundings and whether our view of it is the same for everyone else. You might discover that there is more to this than meets the eye…

What do **you** see in this picture?

Activity

1 On your own, briefly describe what you see in the pictures on the left. What is your experience of them? (Keep it secret!)

2 Now compare your results with a neighbour. Did you see the same thing? Jot down what you agreed and disagreed on.

3 In the 'world out there', the lines on the page are exactly the same for everybody, but some people may have seen very different things in them. Why do you think that is?

4 If a person is colour blind, are they seeing the 'same world' as someone who is not?

5 What does this suggest about the way we see the world? Do we all see the 'same world', or are we seeing different worlds? Is the world created by your mind somehow, as well as 'out there'? Explain your answer with examples or reasons.

Mahatma Gandi : 'As a person thinks *that* they become!' Do you agree with this quote?

Mahatma Gandhi once said: 'As a person thinks, *that* they become.' The words suggest that different kinds of thoughts about myself, and the world around me, lead to different kinds of lives for me in the future. If someone is an **optimist**, for example, then their life may develop in a different way to someone who is a **pessimist**, even if they experience exactly the same things.

Activity

Further activity

1 See if you agree with this idea by thinking about the 'glass of water' example. Will someone who thinks of a glass of water as 'half full' live a happier life than someone who thinks of it as 'half empty'? Why or why not?

2 Are these the only two ways of thinking about the glass with water in it? If you can think of another way, how might that suggest the person views the world in general? Is that way a good way to view the world? (Remember to be thoughtful and give reasons)

3 Do you think we can *choose* to see the world in a certain way?

4 Do you agree with Mahatma Gandhi's comment? Does the way we think about the world affect our future? Explain your answer.

Key Words

Mahatma Gandhi (1869–1948 CE) – *A great spiritual and political leader in India.*

Optimist – *Someone who tends to take the most hopeful view of circumstances.*

Pessimist – *Someone who tends to take the worst view of circumstances.*

Thought diary

Pick one or two thoughts that this unit has made you think about, and jot them down in your Thought diary. They might be questions, ideas, or comments that other people made. It might even be a diagram or picture of some sort. Try http://illusions.specialsite.net for more optical illusions or try and draw one yourself.

Seeing is believing

Do beliefs affect the way we view the world around us?

Imagine that you are a vegetarian; you believe that animals should not be killed for your food. What would you experience if you stood in a butcher's shop? Would it be different from a meat eater's experiences in the same shop? Or imagine that you believe in ghosts; would you experience a power cut during a stormy night in the same way as someone who does not believe in them?

One area that might affect how we view this world, and therefore how we feel, think and act in it, is our beliefs or **convictions**. So how do your beliefs affect *your* life? To help you investigate your own thoughts and understand those of other people, this unit will explore how being a Christian affects their relationship with the world around them.

Activity

Briefly describe how you might a) think; b) feel and c) act in the following situations. Perhaps you could write a few key words down for each one or discuss each case with a neighbour.

a Holding a newly born baby.

b Seeing a TV programme about starving children in a poor country.

c Visiting someone who is dying in hospital.

d Reading about a big company that is cutting down huge areas of rainforest.

e Being a soldier in a war situation.

Further activity

Read carefully through the Christian beliefs and quotes listed below:

- There is an all-powerful, all-knowing, all-good and loving power everywhere in the universe.
- This power or Being, called 'God', made this universe, including you and every other living creature.
- Every human has a 'spark of God' within them, which gives them life, thoughts and feelings.
- This spark, or 'soul', within you will never die, but your body will.
- Humans do not own this universe; they are merely managers of it.
- As managers (or 'stewards'), humans have a responsibility to look after God's creations.
- The Bible and the story of Jesus's life tells humans how to do this; by loving all things.
- If you follow this way of life, your soul will be in Heaven for ever when your body dies.

Bible quotes

And God saw everything that he had made, and, behold, it was very good.

(Genesis 1: 31)

And the Lord God formed man of the dust of the ground, and breathed into his nostrils the breath of life; and man became a living soul.

(Genesis 2: 7)

[Jesus said:] *Thou shall love the Lord thy God with all thy heart, and with all thy soul, and with all thy mind. This is the first and great commandment. And the second is like unto it, thou shall love thy neighbour as thyself.*

(Matthew 22: 37–9)

[Jesus said:] *I am the resurrection, and I am the life; he who believes in me, though he die, yet shall he live, and whoever lives and believes in me shall never die.*

(John 11: 25–6)

[Jesus said:] *Judge not, that ye be not judged. For with what judgement you judge, you shall be judged.*

(Matthew 7: 1–2)

1. Take a moment to imagine that all of these beliefs and quotes are *absolutely true*. Now, how would you a) think; b) feel and c) act in the five activity situations (a–e)?
2. Can you connect some of the quotes to the situations? For example, is there a quote that would make a Christian think or feel or act in a certain way when they see the rainforest being cut down?
3. In groups, discuss whether your personal feelings, thoughts or actions were similar or different to those of a Christian reaction. Would your reactions be different now that you have thought about another viewpoint? Explain your views.
4. Do you think your beliefs *do* affect how you see the world? Can you give an example?

Would an atheist feel and think the same things as a Christian when they see this picture?

Key Words

Conviction – *A firm belief; something thought to be true.*

Thought diary

Add any ideas or questions that this unit has helped you to think about. You might write a poem, or a letter to a Christian expressing your views or perhaps a prayer.

A Buddhist view

Our relationship with the world around us, and with each other, is affected by our beliefs. Even if you do not believe in any particular religion, you still have beliefs that give you a **subjective** (or 'personal') view of life. It is useful to look at other beliefs so that you can see if you agree or disagree with them. You might change your beliefs, or understand why you hold your beliefs more deeply as a result.

Let us investigate another view now, that of the Buddhists. They do not believe in a God, or in a soul, but they do hold beliefs that affect how they view the world and the way they live. Will you agree with their view or not?

Activity

1 On a large piece of paper, draw a small sketch of yourself at the centre of the sheet.

2 In a ring around your sketch, write down at least six things that allow you to be alive in this moment. (clean air? food? health? Think of things that had to happen in the past for you to exist now, as well as things in the present.)

3 In a bigger ring outside your ideas, write down what things in the smaller circle rely on in order to exist. (For 'food', for example, you might put 'good soil' or 'sunlight' for vegetables to grow in.)

4 Discuss your results with others. Think of two statements that you could make about your results. What do they suggest about you and your relationship with other things? Could there be further rings to add outside of the second ring you made? What might that suggest?

5 Do you exist 'separately' from the world, or are you connected to it in some way? Does the 'house of cards' picture give you any ideas?

The Buddhist view

From the everyday view, the world around us seems to be made up of lots of different, separate objects: me here, people over there, tables, chairs, pens, paper… all near each other, but separated. Buddhists agree with this, but think that there are other important things to notice about the *relationship* between things in the world. One view that they hold is, perhaps, similar to ideas you may have found in the activity above. It is called **interdependence**. It means that all things rely on each other for their existence. Things may seem to be separate in one way, but in another they are all connected because they need each other to exist in the first place.

This way of seeing the world encourages Buddhists to treat other living creatures with **compassion**. Buddhists see it as common sense to be kind towards other creatures because each living thing depends on other living things for their own happy existence. If a person harms another, they are increasing everyone's suffering including their own because Buddhists believe that we are all connected in the same stream of events called 'life'.

Activity

Further activity

The Dalai Lama believes in 'interdependence'. Do you agree with that view of the world?

Consider the following. We humans are social beings. We come into the world as the result of others actions. We survive here in dependence on others. Whether we like it or not, there is hardly a moment of our lives when we do not benefit from others activities. For this reason it is hardly surprising that most of our happiness arises in the context of our relationships with others. Nor is it so remarkable that our greatest joy should come when we are motivated by concern for others.

The **Dalai Lama**, *Ethics for the New Millennium*

1 Try to summarize the quote from the Dalai Lama in your own words. (Can you include the word 'interdependence' in your summary?)

2 Do you agree with the Dalai Lama? Can you give examples of where you find happiness through relationships with others?

3 Do you think there is a similarity between the Buddhist idea of being compassionate, and the Christian view of 'loving your neighbour', even though Buddhists do not believe in God? Discuss your views with others and write down any conclusions .

Key Words

Compassion – *Kindness; concern for others.*

Dalai Lama (b.1935) – *A famous Buddhist leader from Tibet.*

Interdependence – *Things rely on each other for their existence.*

Subjective – *Judged from your own point of view.*

Thought diary

Try to explain the idea of Buddhist interdependence in your own words. You could try to express the idea through art or music. Do you agree or disagree with this Buddhist view?

A secular view

A 1995 survey of 13,000 thirteen to fifteen year olds suggested that 61 per cent of teenagers in the UK consider themselves to be **atheist** or **agnostic**.

If a person does not believe in a religion, does that mean that they do not have any beliefs? Are they just a lump of meaningless meat roaming about a world of meaningless objects? Is an atheist or an agnostic just trying to get as much selfish pleasure out of the world as they can, or is the world more meaningful to them than that? This unit will help you to examine non-religious or **secular** views of the world by learning from humanism.

Is there only a life of selfish pleasure if you do not believe in a religion?

Activity

Humanists are people who believe that there is no God or gods, no soul, no afterlife, and that religions do not provide all the answers to life's questions. They do believe, however, that human beings have some powerful abilities, and that they should use these to benefit others as well as themselves. Here are some quotes that express humanist views. Read them carefully, and answer the questions below.

In spite of all the yearnings of men, no one can produce a single fact or reason to support the belief in God and in personal immortality.

Clarence Darrow, defence lawyer in the Monkey Trial (see page 68)

A humanist has four leading characteristics – curiosity, a free mind, belief in good taste, and belief in the human race.

E. M. Forster, British novelist

I do not know what your destiny will be, but one thing I do know: the only ones among you who will be really happy are those who have sought and found how to serve.

Albert Schweitzer, philosopher, awarded the Nobel Peace Prize

Happiness is the only good. The place to be happy is here. The time to be happy is now. The way to be happy is to help make others so.

Robert Ingersoll, American lawyer and orator

As a humanist I believe enhancing human welfare is our primary moral goal. Other goals might include minimizing suffering, making decisions that are fair, and enhancing human freedom and dignity.

Michael Werner, past president of a humanist association

Activity

1 In pairs, using the quotes on the left, write down how a humanist might reply to the following comments:

  a Life must seem so depressing if you do not believe in a religion.

  b Atheists must be selfish because they have no reason to help others.

  c Without God, you are nobody. You cannot really matter in the world.

  d You want to be happy? Look after Number One!

2 Compare your replies with other groups and see if there were any different opinions.

3 How would *you* respond to the comments?

Humanism – a summary

Humanists do not all agree on any one set of particular beliefs. Instead, they believe that each person must try to find their own sense of truth in the world with an open mind. A humanist, therefore, could be said to be a 'free thinker' with a strong sense of moral responsibility towards the world they live in.

Activity

Further activity

1 Religions have symbols that express something very important in their tradition. What symbol would you invent for humanists? You might use ICT or your artistic skills to design one. Add a paragraph of writing to explain why you designed it in that way.

2 Can you find out what the actual humanism symbol is?

Christianity

Buddhism

Islam

Humanism

Key Words

Agnostic – *Someone who believes that you cannot know whether there is a God or not.*

Atheist – *Someone who believes that there is no God.*

Humanist – *A non-religious person who believes in freedom of thought and being 'a good human being'.*

Secular – *Not religious.*

Thought diary

How would you describe 'humanism' to someone who has never heard the word? Jot down your own views about humanism. You might do some research about humanism using the web or library books.

Knowing me

There is one very important relationship that we have for almost every minute of our lives, and yet it may not get much of our attention because it is so close to us; it is the relationship that we have with ourselves. What do we feel or think about ourselves? This unit will help us to find ways of looking at ourselves by learning from the Hindu tradition.

If this represented a person, what would they be like?

Activity

1 One way of exploring our relationship with ourselves is to use our imaginations, so be really creative in this activity. Let your ideas and feelings fly!

- Imagine that your body becomes a landscape of some sort. (It could be anywhere, imaginary or real. Would it be a desert, a city, a forest, a river, caves, or a mixture of these, for example?)
- Imagine that your feelings are a type of weather. What would the temperature of your feelings be like? Are your feelings humid, dry, or rainy weather perhaps?
- Imagine that your mind takes on the form of a living creature of some sort. What creature is your mind like? (It might be human, animal, or completely imaginary.) Where is it in your landscape?
- Close your eyes for a few minutes and imagine each part carefully. Remember to think about your senses too; what would you see, taste, smell, feel and hear?

2 Express the activity above in the best way possible. It might be a poem, a painted or drawn picture, a computer image, a collage, a story, or a piece of music perhaps. It might even be a one-person drama or a dance.

3 What does your image tell you about how you see yourself? Can this view change, and, if so, how?

Looking inside myself – Hinduism and meditation

Hinduism suggests that it is very important to get to know ourselves more deeply. If we do, Hindus believe we can discover that there is much more to us than we might have first imagined. One way of achieving this is to meditate. But what is **meditation**, and why do it?

Hindus believe that our minds are usually so busy 'chattering' with thoughts about the ever-changing outside world that we forget our true identity as the unchanging soul (or **atman**) within. It is rather like being so distracted by the changing clouds that we forget about the big and beautiful sky that is always there as well! In order to learn more about our true nature, we need to calm down our minds and pay close attention to what is really going on within us.

We can achieve this by meditating and there are many different methods of meditation to choose from. Some meditators may concentrate on the sensation of their breath moving in and out of their nostrils, or repeat special sounds (called **mantras**) to themselves. Some Hindus might focus their attention on the 'God within their heart'. Each technique has the same aim; to calm the 'chatty' mind, allowing a person to sense their true nature – their atman – more deeply, and find more peace and happiness as a result.

Activity

Further activity

1 Why might Hindus think it is important to 'know yourself' through meditation?

2 There are at least three other religions that practise meditation. Can you discover which ones they are? Can you find out how one of them practises meditation?

3 Sit comfortably for 30 seconds and see if you can have 'no thoughts at all'. Do you agree with the Hindu view that our minds are 'chatty'?

4 Design a picture or pattern that you think might help you calm your mind by gently focusing on it. What colours, shapes and/or images would you choose?

5 Do you think that keeping your mind quiet would allow you to know more about your 'true self'? Explain your opinion.

Key Words

Atman – *Meaning 'self'; the personal soul or 'true self' that gives life to your body.*

Mantra – *Sacred sounds that are repeated by a meditator to help calm or focus the mind.*

Meditation – *The practice of training the mind, using different methods, to see into the nature of things more deeply and clearly.*

Thought diary

Have you had any new thoughts about how you see yourself today? Do you think that you could change the landscape, the weather or the creature in the first activity, for example? How?

Relating to God

Do you think it would change your life if you did – or did not – believe in God? How? What would change? Billions of people on this planet believe in **theistic religions** (ones that believe there is a God) but why do all of these people believe in something or someone that they cannot see or hear? Where is this God, or proof that He exists? This unit will explore the idea of God, and how one religion describes how humans can have a relationship with God.

Activity

Imagine an alien visits Earth wanting to know about this mysterious being called 'God'. In pairs, create a story about this visit. It might help to think about these areas:

a What should the alien see, or who should the alien ask about God?

b What questions should the alien ask?

c Is there any argument or evidence that might convince the alien that God exists?

d What conclusions does the alien come to about human belief in God?

e What would have to happen for the alien to believe in God?

f Must the alien belong to a religion to believe in God?

You could illustrate the story, or imagine being journalists who want to write an article about the alien's visit.

The Sikh view

There exists but one God, who is called the True, the Creator, free from fear and hate, immortal, ***not begotten, self-existent****, great and compassionate. The True was at the beginning, the True was at the distant past. The True is at the present, O Nanak, the True will be also in the future.*

The beginning of **Guru Nanak's** hymn, recited each morning by Sikhs

Sikhs believe that God cannot be known directly; He is simply too great for our human minds to understand or describe. It is rather like trying to see every bit of the universe at once! Impossible! However, God can be known indirectly through his creations in the form of the real world and all the life within it. By looking at the world, Sikhs can see God 'at work', and learn to appreciate His power and His concern for life. For example, God can be seen indirectly in the beauty of a sunset, in the birth of a baby, in the smile of an old woman, or in the splendour of the stars at night.

Sikhs also believe that they can relate to God through **sewa**, or service to the community. This might take the form of reading the scriptures aloud for others, kind deeds, teaching about Sikhism, or simply washing up after the free communal meal called **langar**. Since Sikhs believe that everyone has a part of God within them, helping other people is very close to having a direct relationship with God. They might also sing hymns, meditate or pray to feel closer to God, and may experience feelings of God's love and care for them awakening in their hearts as a result. He (God) can be realized by **Namsimran** (remembering God's name).

The Sikh tradition of providing the langar.

Activity

Further activity

1 In your own words, try to explain how God can and cannot be known from the Sikh view. (Try to include the words sewa and langar or words from the Sikh hymn on page 14).

2 If God does exist and cannot be known directly, how would you express your feelings towards Him? What kind of actions or thoughts would you use?

3 Do you think it would be a good thing if God did appear to human beings directly? How might it help? What kind of problems might it cause?

4 Pick one other religion and research how followers create a relationship with God. (Do they use prayer, worship, rituals, or images? Is there a particular person who represents God on Earth?)

Key Words

Guru Nanak Dev Ji (1469–1539 CE) – *Indian religious teacher and founder of the Sikh religion.*

Langar – *A free meal provided for everyone, which shows love for others and therefore for God.*

Namsimran – *Remembering God's name.*

Not begotten, self-existent – *Not born from anything before Him; God exists without needing something to cause or produce Him.*

Sewa – *Giving service (in a variety of ways) to the community, an important part of Sikh life.*

Theistic religions – *Religions that believe in God.*

Thought diary

Do you think there is any proof *against* the existence of God? Has this unit changed your views about God at all? How?

Assessment

In this chapter we have begun to explore how we, and others, might relate to the world, people, ourselves and God.

How do *you* see things now? What words would you put on *your* 'lenses'?

Here are a few questions that you might have thought about in each unit:

1. *The world and I – Do we all experience the world in the same way?*
2. *A Christian view – Can beliefs affect our view of the world?*
3. *A Buddhist view – Are we 'separated' from everything else?*
4. *A Humanist view – How might non-religious people see the world?*
5. *A Hindu view – How can I know myself, and why might it be important?*
6. *A Sikh view – How can people know about an invisible God?*

Reflecting on your progress

1. *To help you reflect on what you have learned from this chapter, look back on your work, or in your Thought diary, and write a few lines on each of the following areas, giving reasons to improve your answers:*
   - ⓐ What I enjoyed. Why?
   - ⓑ What I found difficult. Why?

2. *Pick an idea that you liked and try to explain it clearly to another person. Think about:*
   - Where the idea came from.
   - What the idea is about.
   - Why you like the idea.
   - The *best* way to explain it to someone else.

3. *In your Thought diary, copy down five* **skills** *that you have used most during this chapter from the following list:*
   - I listened to others well.
   - I gave reasons for my views.
   - I expressed my ideas clearly.
   - I tried to imagine other people's point of view.
   - I developed my writing or artistic skills.
   - I investigated a new topic well.
   - I made new ideas for myself.
   - I kept on task well.
   - I used lots of imagination.
   - I cared about the feelings of other people.

4. *What facts did you learn? What do you understand now that you did not know about before? Make a spider diagram or poster to show your thoughts.*

Test yourself

1. *Do you think the Christian view of the world is true? Give two reasons why you think it is or is not. [Level 5–AT2]*

2. *Mahatma Gandhi said, 'As a man thinks, that he becomes.' What do you think he meant by that? Do you agree with that comment? [Level 6–AT2]*

3. *'Meditation is just sitting around and doing nothing. It's useless!' How might a Hindu respond to this point of view? [Level 7–AT2]*

4. *What do Buddhists mean by the term 'interdependence'? How does this belief affect their behaviour towards the world around them? Do you see yourself as 'interdependent'? Explain your views. [Level 8–AT2]*

Where next?

1. *Look at the list of skills on this page. Choose two that you want to improve in the future. Perhaps you could note them down in your Thought diary. (Describe two ways in which you could improve them. Is there someone who could give you suggestions? Is there some way of reminding yourself of your aims in future lessons?)*

2. *Think about the topic you enjoyed most. What could you do to investigate it further? Are there any websites or books that could help you find out more?*

3. *Research challenge! See if you can find out how Muslims view the world around them. You might ask Muslims you know, find out on the web, or ask your teacher for ideas. Do Muslims have anything in common with other religions and their views? (Use www.re-xs.ucsm.ac.uk or other websites to help.)*

Well done!

You know more, have thought more and have improved your skills.

KEEP GOING!

What is right and wrong?

This chapter will help you to develop your own views about 'right and wrong' by investigating different opinions, including those of Jainism, Islam, Sikhism and Christianity.

Think about the last good or bad thing that you did. How did you feel afterwards? What was it that made that action 'right' or 'wrong'? Why does it matter? This chapter will help you explore **ethics** – the study of what makes something right or wrong.

Hercules is asked to make a choice between the paths suggested by Virtue (on left) and Pleasure (below right). Are you ever faced with this choice? What do you imagine Hercules is thinking at this moment? Why is Virtue's path 'uphill', and Vice's 'downhill'?

Activity

The moral diamond

1 Here are nine reasons why someone might be discouraged from stealing something that they really want in a local shop. Place them in a diamond grid, with the most powerful reasons not to steal towards the top, and the least powerful reasons lower down.

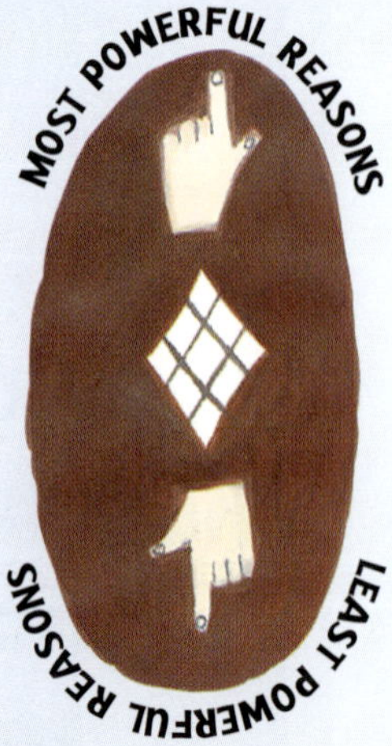

- I don't want to be punished if I get caught.
- I don't like feeling guilty.
- I don't want to make others pay for my actions.
- I don't want to break the law, I might get a record.
- I don't want to disobey an authority (parents, teachers, and so on.)
- I don't want to feel embarrassed if I get caught.
- I don't want to lose other people's respect and trust.
- I don't want to go against the teachings of my religion.
- I don't want the unhappy future that stealing might lead to.

2 Now compare your results with a neighbour. What did you agree or disagree about? Justify your choices with each other by giving reasons for them.

3 What do you think this activity tells you about 'right and wrong'? Does it give you any clues as to where we might get our sense of right and wrong from? Write two statements that summarize your ideas.

Two theories about right and wrong

So, what is it that makes an action right or wrong? For centuries, great thinkers have tried to find an answer to this question. Below are just two possible answers. See if there is one you agree with:

Consequentialists claim that an action is morally right if the **consequence** – or outcome – of the action is of benefit to others. For example, if a person gave money to a charity for the homeless, the consequence is that people who need help will benefit as a result of the action. The action of giving money, therefore, is seen as 'morally right'.

Intentionalists disagree with consequentialists. They claim that an action is right or wrong depending on the **intention** of the person who does it, regardless of what the actual outcome of the action is. If, for example, you go to help a friend with their homework, your intention is to be of benefit to someone else. The action that follows is morally right because the intention is good, even if your friend's homework gets worse as a result of your help!

Activity

Further activity

1 In pairs, write down what a consequentialist and an intentionalist might say about the following situations

a Sam is walking along with Rachel, his new girlfriend, and he is keen to impress her. They are approached by someone collecting money for a school in Africa. He puts 50p in the collection box and grins broadly at Rachel.

b Ahmed spots a blind man about to cross a dangerous road. He runs over to help him. Ahmed trips, knocking the man into the road. An oncoming cement lorry runs over the blind man.

2 Do you think these actions are right or wrong? Must it be one or the other? Give reasons for your opinion.

3 Should actions be judged on consequences or intentions? Are there any alternative ways of judging them?

Key Words

Consequence – *Result or outcome of an action.*

Ethics – *The study of what makes something right or wrong.*

Intentions – *The motives or drives behind an action.*

Thought diary

What other ways might there be of telling whether an action is right or wrong? For example, is an action 'right' only when other people agree it is? Note down any new thoughts that you had.

Motives

No one is perfect; we all do things that are wrong from time to time. But why? Think about the last time you might have lied, been disloyal to someone or taken something you should not have. What were the motives behind the actions? Why did these motives win over your good motives? This unit will help you consider the motives behind wrong actions, and what religions – Sikhism in particular – say about it. Will you agree with their ideas or not?

Activity

1 Find stories of people who have acted immorally, or who have done wrong to others. (You might use newspapers, magazines, news programmes, or examples from your own experience.)

2 Using these examples, discuss why you think the people involved have acted immorally. What drove them to do something wrong? Try to summarize their reasons in single words such as 'greed', 'anger' or 'revenge'.

3 Make a list of as many 'motives for doing wrong' as you can. What are the three worst, or strongest, motives on the list in your view? Give brief reasons for your choices.

DEMONSTRATORS SMASH SHOP WINDOWS IN PROTEST

MADMAN SHOOTS TEN IN RANDOM RESTAURANT RAMPAGE

Thieves steal £50,000 from footballer's home during match

Husband stabs his wife's lover ten times with kitchen knife

The Sikh view

Many religions recognize that wrong actions arise from the wrong motives; anger can lead to active violence, for example, or hatred can lead to cruelty. Here are some religious views about what these bad motives are:

- Sikhs believe that all people fall into one of two categories; those who put God at the centre of their lives are called **gurmukh**, and self-centred people are called **manmukh**. The gurmukh is motivated by the desire to know God more closely, and one way this is achieved is by treating all of God's creations with love, respect and kindness. The manmukh, however, is motivated by selfish desires, aiming to achieve as much personal gain and pleasure for themselves as possible.
- Sikhs identify five main motives that may lead to immoral behaviour and the selfish life of the manmukh. They are lust, anger, greed, emotional attachment (strong desires) and arrogance. Consequently, Sikhs who wish to become gurmukh must strive to reduce the power of these motives so that their actions will serve God, and not themselves. (This can be very difficult! Can you always control your anger or your selfish desires?)

Bad motives in Buddhism – The Three Poisons

Buddhists identify three main causes of **bad karma**, or wrongdoing. They are called the Three Poisons, and are represented in Tibetan Buddhist art as three animals:

The 'Three Poisons' of the mind in Buddhism

Bad motives in Christianity – The Seven Deadly Sins

Christians sometimes refer to the Seven Deadly Sins: Pride, Anger, Envy, Lust, **Gluttony**, **Avarice** and Laziness.

Activity

Further activity

1 Did your list of worst motives match any of the ones mentioned in the religions above? Note them down if they did.

2 Why might it be difficult to lead the life of a gurmukh? Why might a Sikh feel that it is very worthwhile to be a gurmukh?

3 A morality play aims to teach its audience about right and wrong. In groups, create a modern morality play involving motives. Use the information above to help you. You should think about:

- **a** characters with bad, and good, motives behind their actions
- **b** which bad motives you think your audience should learn about
- **c** an ending that teaches the audience a 'moral lesson'; what are the consequences for the bad and good characters as a result of their motives and actions?
- **d** which religion you would represent, or perhaps you could create a humanist (or non-religious) version?

Key Words

Avarice – *Greed for wealth or money.*

Bad karma – *Bad actions that lead to bad results in the future.*

Gluttony – *Greed for pleasure, particularly with regard to food.*

Gurmukh – *In Sikhism, a person who trusts in God and leads a selfless life.*

Manmukh – *In Sikhism, a person who does not trust in God and leads a selfish life.*

Thought diary

Note down any ideas or facts that you found interesting in this unit. In your opinion, which emotion causes the most suffering in the world?

Does it matter?

What do we gain from 'being good' or trying to do 'the right thing'? For example, why should we bother to help a neighbour when we could just concentrate on looking after ourselves? Sometimes 'doing the right thing' means sacrificing what we *want to do* for what we *ought to do*; but what is that sacrifice for?

Religions do not all agree on what right or wrong actions are, but all claim that we will lead better lives if we try to behave in the right way. This unit will explore this claim through the religious ideas of **Jainism**.

Activity

Read the following news broadcast:
[The place: UK. The year: 2016]

New figures released today show that crime and disorder have risen by a dramatic 350 per cent over the last four years. As yet another curfew is imposed – ordering the population to stay indoors from dusk till dawn – the government is forced to consider new ways of solving the moral crisis in our society. Even the new super-prisons are overcrowded, and it is claimed that almost one third of their populations are teenagers…

In pairs or small groups, imagine that the government of 2016 has employed you to help rescue the country from its moral decline. What could you do to persuade people that it is worth being a good, moral citizen? Think about:

a How you could communicate your ideas (posters, TV, websites, films).

b What are the advantages of people behaving in a good, moral way? (Think of advantages to everyone and to the individual: less fear? better business? and so on.)

c What images or messages might persuade people to think about their actions and their consequences?

The Jain view

A diagram of the universe

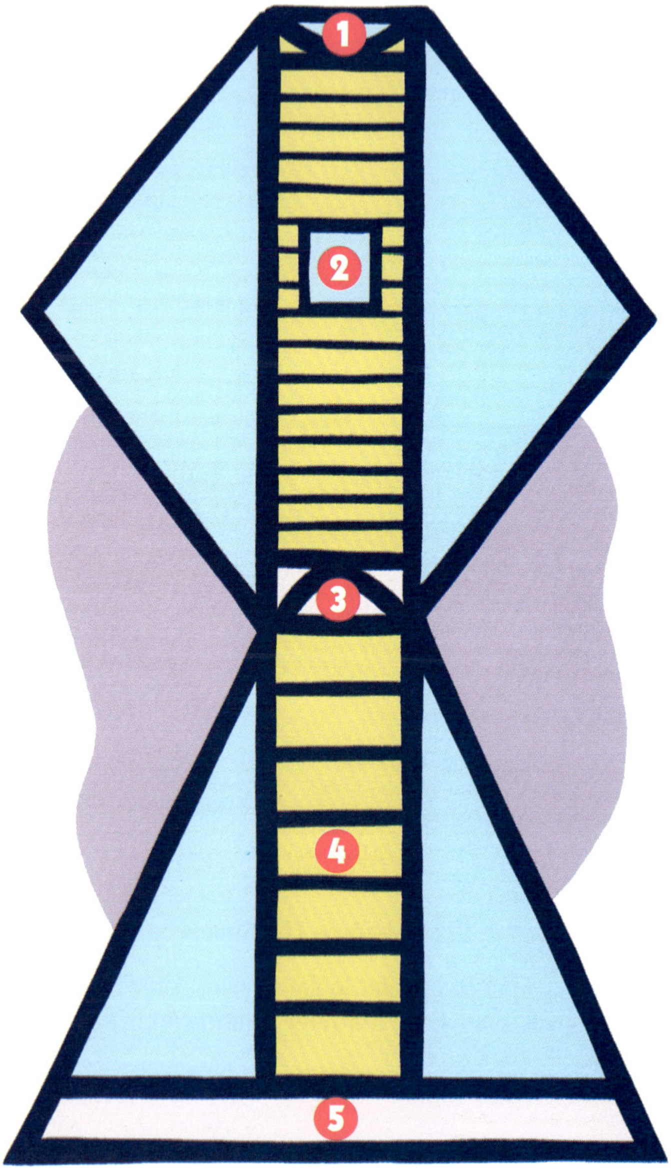

Humans are in the middle ❸ with heavenly areas above and hellish areas below. Good deeds allow the **jiva** to float upwards (towards ❶) bad deeds weigh the jiva down (towards ❺)

Jains believe that humans must strive to act morally both for their own, personal benefit, and the benefit of all living things. They believe that our actions now will affect not only this life, but our future lives through reincarnation as well. If we act badly ('bad karma'), by not respecting other life, we will experience more suffering in our future as a result. If we act with good intentions and love for other beings, everyone will benefit.

Jains also believe that we are really a soul called a jiva. The jiva is the true and everlasting part of a human being that moves from life to life through reincarnation. It is the life force or 'true self' that feels, experiences and expresses life. Our jiva is thought to be 'weighed down' by our bad deeds, keeping it in a low part of the Jain universe where there is more suffering. However, good actions can help to free our true nature, allowing it to float up to the top of the universe where it may enjoy perfect peace and happiness.

Jain monks often wear covers over their mouths and sweep the path in front of them to prevent them from killing insects (an act of bad karma).

Activity

Further activity

1 Design a diagram or picture of the universe that would illustrate the Jain ideas. Show how:

  a good karma lightens the soul in the universe, and

  b how bad karma weighs it down, causing more suffering.

Label the diagram with arrows and words like 'good karma', 'bad karma', 'jiva', 'more suffering' and 'more happiness'.

2 Jot down any phrases that we use in everyday language that use this idea of 'low' and 'high' to express happiness or sadness. (Helpful hints: 'I'm weighed down by work', or 'He said it with a heavy heart', and so on.) Do you think that we are really talking about our souls in these cases?

Key Words

Jainism – *An Indian religion founded by Mahavira about 2500 years ago.*

Jiva – *The Jain term for the life force within all living things. Jains aim to free their jiva from the prison of the body.*

Thought diary

Do you think that acting morally now will lead you to a better life? How will it be 'better'? Try to give a few examples. Add any ideas that this unit made you think about.

But what is right?

When you think that something is right, do you think that it is right for everybody, or is it right *just for you*? For example, if you think that being a vegetarian is morally right, does that mean that all meat-eaters are wrong, or do they simply have a different opinion about what is right? If you think that the treatment of the Jews (the Holocaust) during World War II was wrong, is that just your personal view, or should everyone think that it was wrong?

This unit will help you to work out whether your sense of right and wrong should be the same for everyone.

Activity

1 Put the following actions into one of two categories: 'This should be totally banned for everybody' (**absolute morality**) or 'This should be a matter of personal opinion' (**relative morality**).

- Torture
- Smoking cigarettes
- Suicide
- The death penalty
- Drinking alcohol
- Smacking children
- Smoking cannabis
- Rape
- Gambling
- Abortion
- Boxing
- Killing in war
- Eating meat
- Having sex at fourteen years old.

2 Compare your results with others. Did you agree on everything? Explain any differences of opinion you had with each other.

3 Using your results, what can you say about moral actions? Are some a matter of opinion (relative)? Do you think some are wrong no matter who you are (absolute)? Write two sentences about your results.

Islam, the Qur'an, and morality

A Muslim reads the Qur'an, the holy book of Islam

What does 'doing the right thing' mean to a Muslim? Is it just a matter of their personal opinion, or are there acts that all Muslims regard as right or wrong?

One of the most important guides to moral behaviour for a Muslim is their holy book called the **Qur'an**. Its 114 surahs (or 'chapters') contain many statements about what is right and wrong. For example, it tells Muslims not to have sex outside of marriage, gossip, kill without just cause, be wasteful, or treat parents disrespectfully. Muslims should also always keep their promises, be humble, pray to God, and treat others with respect and kindness.

For Muslims, this is more than just friendly advice because the Qur'an is regarded as the word of Allah; it is Allah – God, the Creator of all life – that is stating what is right and wrong here. Therefore 'doing the right thing' for a Muslim means following the commands of Allah as described in the Qur'an; it is not just a matter of personal opinion. If God has said that drinking alcohol or lying is wrong, then it is absolutely wrong for Muslims. The challenge for Muslims is to see how closely they can obey the words and wishes of Allah.

Muslims also believe that the intention behind their actions is very important. If they make a mistake, they trust in Allah's mercy and forgiveness, but they should always try to have a good heart behind all that they do:

> *God will not call you to account for thoughtlessness in your oaths, but for the intention in your hearts; and God is Oft-forgiving, Most Forbearing*
>
> Surah 2: 225

Activity

1 Do some research on the Qur'an or the **Hadith**. Try to find any advice to Muslims on how to act in the 'right' way.

2 If you believed in a book that reliably listed what right and wrong actions were, how would you use it to help you? Would it be easier to be good person, or more difficult? Give a reason for your views.

3 Do you think there can only be one sense of right and wrong, or can there be many?

Key Words

Absolute morality – *There is only one set of 'right or wrong' actions that should apply to everyone.*

Hadith – *Muslim holy book containing the words, actions and instructions of Muhammad (pbuh).*

Qur'an – *The holy book of Islam, containing the words of Allah as revealed to Muhammad (pbuh) about 1,400 years ago.*

Relative morality – *What is right and wrong depends on the views of different people.*

Thought diary

What did this unit make you wonder about? Have your ideas about right and wrong changed? Jot your own thoughts down as clearly as possible.

The Golden Rule – a good rule?

How do you feel when you meet someone for the first time? Nervous? Curious to see what they are like? Wondering whether they will like you or not? Perhaps they are feeling the same! But how should you treat each other? Is there any guidance religions might give us? This unit will help you to explore moral behaviour towards other people through one particular guideline that religions seem to have in common.

Activity

1 Imagine you are in the situations below. Discuss each situation with a neighbour, and make a choice of 'yes' or 'no' in each case.

You are:

a a fifteen-year-old girl and you discover that you are pregnant. You do not feel ready to be a mother. Would you have an abortion?

b a prison officer who needs to get information about a kidnapped child from a prisoner who refuses to speak to you. Would you torture the person in order to get it?

c walking past a homeless person who is asking for spare change. He is the sixth homeless person you have seen today. Would you give him money?

d a judge sentencing a person who killed 500 people in a bomb attack. The law in your country allows the death penalty. Would you order the murderer to be executed?

e someone whose best friend has a terminal disease with very little hope of a cure. They are in a lot of pain and ask you to switch off their life support machine. Would you do it?

2 Share your answers as a group. Did everyone agree on what to do, or were there differences?

3 In which cases do you feel *certain* that you did the right thing? What does this tell you about making moral decisions?

Golden rules

Almost all religions in the world today seem to agree on one key idea about how we should try to treat others. In Christianity, this idea is known as **The Golden Rule**:

Do to others what you would have them do to you.

Matthew 7: 12

Other religions express this same idea in slightly different ways:

Buddhism

Hurt not others in ways that you yourself would find hurtful.

Udana-Varga 5: 18

Hinduism

This is the essence of all duty: do nothing unto others which would cause you pain if done to you.

Mahabharata 5: 1517

Islam

Not one of you is a believer until he loves for his brother what he loves for himself.

Fourth Hadith of an-Nawawi 13

Jainism

A man should wander about treating all creatures as he himself would be treated.

Sutrakritanga 1.11.33

Judaism

What is hateful to you, do not to your fellow man. This is the law: all the rest is commentary.

Talmud, Shabbat 31a

Sikhism

No one is my enemy, none a stranger and everyone is my friend.

Guru Arjan Dev: AG 1299

Every religion emphasizes human improvement, love, respect for others, sharing other people's suffering. On these lines every religion had more or less the same viewpoint and the same goal.

The Dalai Lama

Activity

Further activity

1 Test the Golden Rule out. Go back to the situations given on page 26, and ask:

- **a** Could I apply the Golden Rule here?
- **b** If I can, what would the Golden Rule suggest I should do?

2 Has the Golden Rule changed any of your answers? Do you think it is a good rule to follow?

3 As a group, see if you can invent a situation when you think that the Golden Rule should *not* be followed. Challenge other groups with your situation and see what they would do.

4 If you could create a Golden Rule that everyone should follow, what would it be? How would you phrase it exactly?

Key Words

The Golden Rule – *A common guideline for how we should treat other people (sometimes called the 'Ethic of Reciprocity').*

Thought diary

See if you can find examples of the Golden Rule being followed or broken, and make a collage or collection of them in your diary (TV, newspapers, magazines, examples from your own life). You might add any ideas that this unit made you think about.

Justice

How should people who have done wrong be treated? If you hit someone, should you be hit back? When should you be understanding and forgive others for doing wrong? When have you been punished and did you think it was fair? This unit is about justice and wrongdoing; what is a fair way of treating people who do wrong, and what does Christianity have to say about this?

Activity

Be a judge!

Imagine that the following individuals have been found guilty of these crimes. In pairs, give each one a specific 'sentence'. *Any kind* of punishment is allowed, but you must make it as fair as possible!

a James: 19, supplied ecstasy tablets to two 15 year olds; one died in hospital as a result.

b Vicky: 25, murdered her husband while he was asleep. He had been physically violent towards her since their marriage three years ago.

c Garth: 42, bombed an enemy army barracks, and was captured soon after. Thirteen soldiers and two visiting civilians died in the attack.

d Kumar: 75, stopped by police in his car on a routine check, and found to be well over the legal alcohol limit.

e Sasha: 13, stole £40 from a school charity fund.

Share your 'sentences', and the reasons for them, in small groups. Discuss whether they are fair to i) the criminal and their family; ii) the victims and their families; iii) the community as a whole. If you had done those crimes, would you accept your own sentence as a 'fair' one? Did people's ages make any difference? Did forgiveness and understanding play any part in sentencing these people?

A Christian view

Christians find many references to justice in the Bible, and use these to help them make decisions in real life. The **Old Testament** contains rules that were made before Jesus was alive, and some are very different to the teachings of Jesus in the **New Testament**. Compare them for yourselves.

The Old Testament

...thou shall give life for life, eye for eye, tooth for tooth, hand for hand, foot for foot, burning for burning, wound for wound, stripe for stripe.

(Exodus 21: 24–5)

He that spares the rod hates his son: but he that loves him is careful to discipline him.

(Proverbs 13: 24)

Withhold not discipline from a child: for if you beat him with the rod, he shall not die. Thou shall beat him with the rod, and shall save his soul from Hell.

(Proverbs 23: 13–14)

The New Testament

Ye have heard that it hath been said 'An eye for an eye, and a tooth for a tooth: But I say unto you, That ye resist not evil: but whosoever shall strike thee on thy right cheek, turn to him the other also.

(Matthew 5: 38–9)

...I say unto you, Love your enemies, bless them that curse you, do good to them that hate you, and pray for them which despitefully use you, and persecute you.

(Matthew 5: 44)

Master [Jesus], this woman was taken in **adultery***, in the very act. Now Moses in the law commanded us that such a one should be stoned; but what sayest thou?... [Jesus replies] He that is without sin among you, let him cast the first stone at her.*

(John 8: 4–7)

Is physical punishment a fair or good form of punishment?

Activity

Further activity

Using the information on this page, try to answer these questions:

1. What do the Old Testament quotes suggest about how wrongdoers should be treated?
2. What do the quotes from the New Testament suggest about punishment?
3. Imagine two schools; one has a punishment system based on the Old Testament quotes, and the other on the New Testament. How would people behave in each school? Which school would you prefer to be in, and why?

Key Words

Adultery – *Having sex with someone who is not your wife/husband when you are already married.*

New Testament – *The second part of the Bible, particularly important to Christians because it describes Jesus's life and teachings.*

Old Testament – *The first and larger part of the Bible based on events before Jesus's life.*

Thought diary

Have you had any new ideas about how 'wrongdoers' should be treated? Can you think of a useful guideline or phrase? Jot down any thoughts or feelings that you have.

Assessment

In this chapter we have begun to think about ethics and how it might affect our lives in different ways.

Here are a few questions that you might have thought about in each unit:

1. *About ethics – What makes an action right or wrong?*
2. *A Sikh view – Why do people do bad things?*
3. *A Jain view – Why bother about being good?*
4. *A Muslim view – Is there only one sense of 'right' in the world?*
5. *The Golden Rule – Is there moral advice that everyone should follow?*
6. *A Christian view – What is fair punishment?*

Do you think killing someone can ever be a fair form of punishment? Does anyone else suffer as a result of this punishment?

Reflecting on your progress

1. *To help you reflect on what you have learned from this chapter, look back on your work, or in your Thought diary, and write a few lines on each of the following areas, giving reasons to improve your answers:*
   a. What I enjoyed. Why?
   b. What I found difficult. Why?
2. *Pick an idea that you liked and try to explain it clearly to another person. Think about:*
   - Where the idea came from.
   - What the idea is about.
   - Why you like the idea.
   - The *best* way to explain it to someone else.
3. *In your Thought diary, copy down five **skills** that you have used most during this chapter from the following list:*
   - I listened to others well.
   - I gave reasons for my views.
   - I expressed my ideas clearly.
   - I tried to imagine other people's point of view.
   - I developed my writing or artistic skills.
   - I investigated a new topic well.
   - I made new ideas for myself.
   - I kept on task well.

- I used lots of imagination.
- I cared about the feelings of other people.

4. *What facts did you learn? What do you understand now that you did not know about before? Make a spider diagram or poster to show your thoughts.*

Test yourself

1. *Is 'right and wrong' just a matter of personal opinion? Try to give examples of when it might and might not be personal choice. (Hint: Pages 24 and 25 might help!) [Level 5–AT2]*
2. *Jesus taught that we should not take revenge, but 'love our enemies' instead. Give your opinion about this advice and say what a Christian might think about it. [Level 6–AT2]*
3. *Is The Golden Rule a good rule that should always be followed? Give your own reponse, and one other response to this question. [Level 7–AT2]*
4. *Explain why Jains believe in 'ahimsa' (non-violence). Add whether you agree with their views about karma and the jiva. [Level 8–AT2]*

Where next

1. *Look at the list of skills on this page. Choose two that you want to improve on in the future. Perhaps you could note them down in your Thought diary. (Perhaps you chose two skills to improve in an earlier chapter; have they improved? How can you tell?)*
2. *Think about the topic you enjoyed most. What could you do to investigate it further? Are there any websites or books that could help you find out more?*
3. *Can you find out what Judaism has to say about people who do wrong? What does 'doing wrong' mean to Jewish believers? (Try www.re-xs.ucsm.ac.uk).*

Well done!

You know more, have thought more and have improved your skills. KEEP GOING!

Power play

What is 'power'? Who or what has 'power'? Is power good or bad, right or wrong, friend or foe?

We humans can think about power as an idea, and also experience and exhibit power-behaviour in many ways.

This chapter will help you investigate different types of power and consider who and/or what has power by focusing on Aboriginal ideas, Judaism, Hinduism and Christianity.

Activity

Monkey business

Apes and chimpanzees use power-behaviour much like ours. Read the following observations aloud in class. Three people could later act it out.

Everard and Goliath are chimps. They get into a fight. Goliath beats up Everard.

However, Everard does not run away but follows Goliath. When Goliath stops, a trembling Everard, bleeding and screaming in pain, presents his backside to Goliath. After a few moments the mighty Goliath accepts this acknowledgement of his **dominant** status and pats Everard's back.

Whenever Goliath or Everard meet a half-grown chimp, the less powerful creature submits to them in some way or other. Cheeky Charlie, a baby chimp, on the other hand shows them no respect. Despite this lack of respect, Goliath and Everard are friendly to Charlie. However, when Goliath gets excited by some new event – in this case a sudden thunderstorm – he immediately changes his attitude toward Charlie and tosses the youngster out of his path like a stick.

Everard follows Goliath as lightning and thunder crack open the sky. They race full-speed down the slope, hooting with excitement, breaking branches from trees, waving them in the air, and hurling them ahead. When they get to the bottom, they plod back up to the top, repeating their performance a number of times. What are they doing? Why are these practical creatures doing something so seemingly impractical? Some **zoologists** believe that the chimps find meaning in the forces of nature around them, giving them energy and a feeling of **power**. It is the **non-verbal** equivalent of: 'I'm part of a greater power in the sky!'

Activity

1 Read Monkey business again. As you read, ask yourself how do Goliath and Everard respond to power? Write down any thoughts you have.

2 Write a magazine article for a teenage audience about what you have read so far about power behaviour. The following questions will help you write your article:

- Is power fearsome? Why does Everard follow Goliath? Does he feel better for having done so?
- Why do you think Goliath behaves like he does with Charlie?
- How does Goliath a) show compassion; b) demand respect and c) sense powers beyond himself?
- By reading about the behaviour of chimpanzees, what have you learnt about power?
- Can you think of any similar ways that you and other human beings deal with power? Give some examples.

3 **The God of Power**

Power is defined as: 'the ability to act on a person or thing'.

Most religions acknowledge higher powers that must be obeyed, revered and worshipped. In the Jewish Bible (the Tenakh) one of God's names is Shadai, who is the Storm God, or God of Power. The God of Power is depicted as:

- a **transcendent** Being, demanding obedience, with severe penalties for disobedience
- a loving and compassionate Being
- a Being who has a personal relationship with those who revere him.

Who, or what, if anything, meets these requirements/characteristics of power. Make a list, compare your list with your neighbours.

Activity

Further activity

1 How have you experienced power? Think of gestures or language you use to show power or react to power? Express them in a one-person drama.

2 Hens exhibit power-behaviour in a 'pecking order'. The winner in a fight thereafter can lord over the lesser creatures. Can you think of examples when humans behave, or have behaved, in a similar fashion?

3 What similarities if any, can you see between Shadai, the God of Power, and Goliath?

4 Jot down any ideas you have about the following. Do humans ideas of higher powers come from: a) society's power structures; b) our need to come to terms with the power of nature or c) the 'higher power' itself?

Key Words

Dominant – *Occupying a more powerful commanding position.*

Non-verbal – *Communication without words.*

Power – *The ability to act on a person or thing.*

Revered – *Gives great respect or admiration.*

Shadai – *Hebrew storm-God, God of Power.*

Tenakh – *The Jewish Bible.*

Transcendent – *Something that goes far beyond ordinary limits.*

Zoologist – *A scientist who studies the animal kingdom.*

Thought diary

There are different levels of power. What powers, if any, do you look up to? Pick any question that has made you think differently about power and write down your views about it.

The elements – friend or foe?

This unit will help you consider the power of the elements by exploring Aboriginal beliefs about the **environment**.

- The largest tidal wave ever recorded travelled at 350 mph across the Indian Ocean and produced huge 300 ft high waves.
- The Sun's temperature at the surface is 5,530 °C. (9,980 °F). At the centre it is 15,000,000 °C. (27,000,000 °F).
- A hurricane contains more energy than all the nuclear weapons in the world.
- An earthquake like the one in Chile in 1960, recorded on the Richter Scale at 9.5, made over 2 million people homeless.

The **elements** – fire, earth, air and water – can fill us with **awe** and fear. Planet Earth is an incredible combination of elemental forces at work. We are made from it, controlled by it, and depend on it.

Activity

Mother Earth

1 Read the poem opposite. Express how this poem makes you feel in a drawing/collage or a piece of artwork.

2 Read the poem again. Which element is not mentioned?

3 Write your own poem about any one of the four elements. Include ideas about how it is a healing power as well as a destructive power.

4 If you want to, present your poem in the shape of the element of your choice.

If the Earth
were only a few feet in diameter,
floating a few feet above a field somewhere,
people would come from everywhere to marvel
at it. People would walk around it marvelling at its
big pools of water, its little pools and the water flowing
between. People would marvel at the bumps on it and the
holes in it. They would marvel at the very thin layer of gas
surrounding it and the water suspended in the gas. The people
would marvel at all the creatures walking around the surface of
the ball and at the creatures in the water. The people would
declare it as sacred because it was the only one, and they would
protect it so that it would not be hurt. The ball would be the
greatest wonder known, and people would come to pray to
it, to be healed, to gain knowledge, to know beauty and to
wonder how it could be. People would love it and defend
it with their lives because they would somehow
know that their lives could be nothing without it.
If the Earth were only a few feet in diameter.

Joe Miller

Fire, water…

The spark!

Religions understand the importance of the elements in our lives; after all, we are made up of them, and they are seen as being linked to higher powers. Though the elements have a wild, untameable quality, religions teach that they are also forces for life and healing.

Australia, the land of fire, is the driest continent on Earth and fire is the element that has shaped the land and its people for centuries. Bush fires in Australia can be terrifyingly powerful. The tribal communities of Australia, the **Aborigines**, have lived with the awesome threat of fire for 60,000 years, and they have learnt how to use the element. They realize its powers of **rejuvenation** and, by burning land in small, contained fires, they remove the risk of destructive bush fires and are able to preserve a balanced environment.

Activity

Further activity

Aboriginal culture is strongly linked to the element of fire, with its power to create as much as destroy. In this land of baking sun and bushfires, the story of creation, called the **Dreamtime**, is a story of fire:

> *In the early Dreamtime, the creatures of the world did not look as they do today. The Father examined them and said, 'You are not a proper people and not proper animals. We must change this'. With his firestick he lit a ceremonial fire that spread until it encompassed the world. It swept over all creatures. It burned the earth and the stones. After the fire had passed, the creatures and the humans took their present form and character.*

1 What does this story tell you about the power of fire? Write your own fire creation story.

2 Think about ways in which the elements can heal us. Find an example of a religion using the power of an element to help or heal (for example, Hindus bathing in the River Ganges).

Key Words

Aborigines – *Collective name for the first peoples of Australia.*

Awe – *Feeling of respect mixed with wonder and fear.*

Dreamtime – *Creation story of the Aborigines.*

Elements – *Powers of nature.*

Environment – *Surroundings, surrounding objects, region, conditions or influences.*

Rejuvenation – *To become young again.*

Thought diary

Think about these statements: 'We should respect the elements'; 'We are forever at the mercy of the elements'; 'We can make use of the elements to help us'.

The problem of evil

Pick out one of these questions, and, in rough, note down any ideas or answers that come to mind:

- Why do people suffer from natural disasters, horrible diseases, predators and poisonous plants?
- Why do humans suffer because of the actions of other human beings?
- Why are innocent people allowed to be hurt?
- How can anyone believe in a loving God when so many humans and animals suffer?

God and evil

If you were an all-powerful (**omnipotent**) God, would you get rid of evil in the world? In fact, given the opportunity, maybe you would never have allowed evil in the first place?

For many people the existence of evil in the world is a stumbling block for faith in God. If we allow that God is weak or evil then there is no problem. However many religious believers do not believe in a weak or evil God but an all powerful and all loving God. But how can this be so when evil exists? This unit will help you explore your own thoughts about this question by looking at some possible solutions to the **problem of evil**.

Activity

1 To start with, have a class vote on whether people believe in an all powerful and all loving God.

2 Read the following conversation between Aicha and Dave. They have just watched a news report about refugees:

AICHA: If God is supposed to be loving and powerful, why does He let it happen?

DAVE: God? What's God got to do with it?

AICHA: Well, if God is supposed to be all-powerful, He must be able to stop horrible things happening.

DAVE: But surely these refugees are victims of man not God? After all, it was men who started the wars.

AICHA: But if God created the world, why did He not create people who didn't fight?

DAVE: Human beings are free to choose between good and evil. If they had no choice, they'd be like robots.

AICHA: But there'd be no pain?

DAVE: It wouldn't work. In a world without difficulties there'd be nothing to struggle against.

3 In pairs, try to continue the conversation. Make a record of what you say.

4 Here are some arguments that some people might use in an attempt to solve the problem of evil. Can you use any of them in your conversation?

Which ones do you think are good arguments? Are there any that are unconvincing? Rank them in order of what you consider to be the best argument down to the weakest argument:

- Evil is caused by human selfishness.
- God grants a certain amount of freedom to humans, and this freedom inevitably results in evil. If you had no choice but to be good, would this mean that 'Heaven' was 'Hell'?
- What may seem like evil, for example, young children drowning in floods, is not actually 'evil', but one of the hazards of life on Earth.
- God works in mysterious ways and people suffer for reasons that are beyond human understanding.
- Suffering is a challenge, because its energy can be transformed into something positive. Suffering is built into the birth process of the world.
- After death, all the suffering of this world will be forgotten in the joy of a new life.
- Suffering is a form of punishment.

Activity

1 Discuss the following questions with a friend. Afterwards prepare a survey on the 'problem of evil'. Write down some questions to ask your family.

- What is evil?
- Where does evil come from?
- Is evil 'inside' or 'outside' of us?
- Are people born evil?
- Can people become evil?
- Are animals evil?
- Would evil exist in the world even without human beings?

Key Words

Omnipotent – *All-powerful.*

Problem of evil – *The presence of evil in the world suggests to some people that the creator God cannot be both all powerful and all loving.*

Thought diary

Ask your questions to at least three people. Did you find anything out? Have people's views changed since the class vote at the beginning?

Human power

Think about times when you have felt creative and other times when you have felt destructive. What caused you to feel like this?

As a species we have the power to create, invent and discover many things about the world around us.

So what are we: creators, destroyers or both? This unit will help you explore human power by investigating the Jewish view about human nature and responsibilities.

Love of power is the demon of men. Let them have everything – health, food, a place to live, entertainment – they are and remain unhappy and low-spirited: for the demon waits and waits and will be satisfied.
Friedrich Nietzsche, philosopher (1844–1900)

The release of atom power has changed everything except our way of thinking. I wish I'd been a watchmaker instead.
Albert Einstein, physicist (1879–1955)

Man is the bad child of the universe.
Robert Oppenheimer, scientist (1904–67)

Religious ideas have sprung from the need for humans to defend themselves against the crushing power of nature.
Sigmund Freud, psychoanalyst (1865–1939)

We have guided missiles and misguided men.
Dr Martin Luther King, Civil Rights leader (1929–68)

The power of man has grown in every sphere, except over himself.
Sir Winston Churchill, British politician (1874–1965)

Man is the only animal that goes forth in cold blood and calmly slaughters strangers of his own species.
Mark Twain, writer (1835–1910)

Activity

1 Pick any one quote from this page. Illustrate your choice with a poster/sketch/cartoon or book cover design.

2 What does the quote you have chosen tell you about human power? Share any thoughts you have with the rest of the class.

3 An alien visiting Earth wants to know is 'MAN' friend or foe?

In small groups, produce a short sketch about the visit. It might help to think about these questions:

- **a** Where would you go to show the alien examples of 'MAN' power? (The alien has a time machine so you can go back in history too.)
- **b** Who would you go to find out more about 'MAN's' power (for example, a scientist, a politician, a religious person, a historian, a psychologist)?
- **c** What questions should the alien ask about 'MAN' power?
- **d** On returning home, the alien has to give a talk to other aliens, called 'MAN – friend or foe?' Write down what the alien might say. What questions might the audience ask?
- **e** Imagine after meeting the alien it has taken you to give a talk on the aliens planet. Your talk is called 'friend or foe?' what would you say about your race – the human race? Write ten key ideas to help you. What questions might the audience ask you?

The Jewish view

> *So God created man in his own image, in the image of God he created him; male and female he created them. And God blessed them, and God said to them, 'Be fruitful and multiply, and fill the earth and subdue it; and have dominion over the fish of the sea and over the birds of the air and over every living thing that moves upon the Earth'.*
>
> Genesis 1: 27–8

Judaism teaches that all power comes from the highest power, God. Humans are created in the 'image of God'. Humans are unique in creation because of **free will**: free to make choices and have the intelligence and wisdom to distinguish between the power of good and evil:

> *I have set before you life and death, blessing and cursing: choose, therefore, life.*
>
> Deuteronomy 11: 26

Jews remember the story of God destroying humanity in a terrible flood after people had chosen 'death', the power of evil. Noah, a 'righteous man', is chosen by God to survive the flood to start the human race anew and to live by the seven Commandments known as the **Noahide Code**, or the **sheva mitzvoth**.

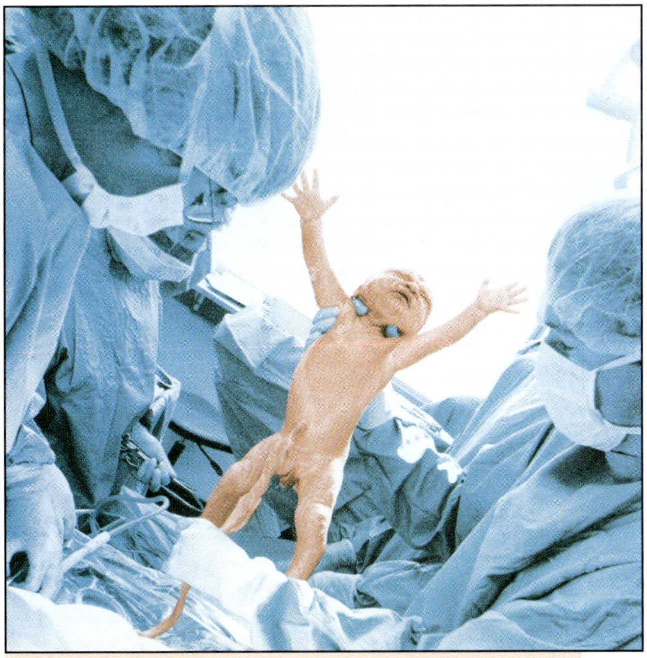

Created in the image of God?

For Jews, power and responsibility are inseparable. One without the other leads to destruction. We are placed at the head of creation as **stewards** to protect the Earth and all her living things. We are temporary caretakers, not owners of God's creation.

Activity

Further activity

1 How do you think the idea of being made in God's image affects a Jewish person's:
   - **a** thoughts
   - **b** feelings
   - **c** actions about the environment?

2 Look at the quotes in this unit. Might a Jewish person agree or disagree with them?

3 Do you have to be religious to believe that we are made 'in the image' of something higher than ourselves? Could an atheist view 'man' as the **pinnacle** of creation? Give reasons for your answers.

4 Read the full story of Noah in Genesis 6,7,8. Design a book cover on any aspect of the story you want to or write a poem, song or rap about the story.

Key Words

Free will – *The ability to choose one's actions.*

Noahide Code – *The seven laws given to Noah by God.*

Pinnacle – *The highest point.*

Sheva mitzvoth – *The seven commandments of Noah.*

Stewards – *Caretakers who look after land or property.*

Thought diary

Find out what seven commandments are in the Noahide Code. Make up your own 'seven commandments' or rules that you would want if you were stranded on a desert island with twenty other people.

Body power

It has been estimated that if its chemical elements had to be bought on the open market, a human body would cost at least six million pounds!

Achievements in sport push back the frontiers of bodily achievements – running and swimming ever faster, jumping ever further and higher, lifting heavier weights.

But when you play sport, is it just a physical activity?

Is winning the aim of sport?

If all your attention is on winning, do you actually stop playing well?

Sport has been called a 'laboratory for experimenting with bodily power'. In this unit by exploring Hindu ideas we will consider whether body power is the most important power that we possess.

Did you know?

The human body can live in extremes of temperatures, display massive strength and stamina, and develop amazing skills. It is a mini chemical factory with 30 trillion cells (eighteen noughts) performing about 10,000 chemical functions.

Activity

1 Make a list of some physical human achievements in water, on land, on ice, in space, in heat or cold, of artistic grace (for example, ballet dancing).

2 Now make a list of what you feel are your own top three physical achievements. Organize these different achievements into groups based on whether they were exhibitions of courage, endurance, skill or strength.

3 Discuss the following questions with a neighbour and write down some of your ideas:

- **a** Do these achievements only involve the body?
- **b** Are these achievements possible without the concentration of your mind?
- **c** What is most powerful – the body or the mind?
- **d** Can the body fulfil its potential without the mind?
- **e** What qualities of mind do athletes or ballet dancers need to perform to the top of their abilities?

Spiritual athletes

Hindus believe that by properly directing the power of the body and the power of the mind they can free themselves from the process of reincarnation which binds them to the cycle of repeated birth and death. This practice is called **yoga**. The word 'yoga' comes from *yuj*, a Sanskrit word (an ancient Indian language) related to the English 'yoke', meaning 'to unite' or 'to join together'. The origin of the word 'religion' has much the same meaning: 'to bind together'. In the West, yoga is often presented as a series of physical exercises, but for Hindus yoga is a powerful spiritual practice leading to total liberation of the self from the entanglement of matter.

Thus let the athlete of the spirit be constant in integrating himself, his mind restrained; then will he approach that peace… which lives in Me.
Bhagavad Gita 6: 10–15

In the Hindu scriptures called the Yoga Sutras, there are eight stages of yoga:

1 Avoiding negative habits and qualities, for example, violence, laziness.

2 Developing positive habits and qualities, for example, self-discipline.

3 Adopting 'right' postures (**asana**).

4 Concentrating on breathing exercises – to help control and purify the mind.

5 Turning the senses inwards – withdrawing the mind from outside influences.

6 Mastering concentration to focus attention on a single object, in the moment.

7 Meditating to allow an uninterrupted flow of attention to the mind.

8 A state of higher consciousness sometimes referred to as a state of 'pure seeing', of insight, and illumination (**Samadhi**).

Activity

Further activity

1 Are there any activities you do that use these techniques? Think about what it means to:

a focus your attention on one object

b resist the urge to quit

c do something for the pleasure of doing it rather than the 'goal'.

2 Stand up and put your arms out straight either side of you. Keep completely still. Do not move or talk. Hold them there for two minutes, if you can. Is physical achievement only about movement? Did your mind play any part in keeping your arms still?

Key Words

Asana – *Posture, the third stage of yoga involving physical excercises.*

Samadhi – *A state of higher awareness; 'pure seeing' and insight.*

Yoga – *A Hindu spiritual practice that releases us from the cycle of rebirth.*

Thought diary

Observe any physical activities you do over the next week and consider if the body needs the mind to achieve its full potential.

The power of silence

HUSH! Listen! Be silent for 30 seconds. What do you hear? Complete silence? Background noise? Inner chattering?

Silence can be frightening. Hostages and prisoners have been kept in **solitary confinement**, spending years alone in a silent cell. People have been kept in silence and denied expression of their thoughts or opinions.

But is silence scary or can it give you power? This unit will explore what some Christians think about silence and how it might affect their lives.

Silence is scary.

Noise is 'unwanted sound'.

Activity

1 Has silence ever taken your power away – maybe a time spent alone in a very quiet place, or sitting silently in a car or a room with somebody else and feeling uncomfortable, nervous, awkward? Jot down your thoughts.

2 Read the following sayings about silence:

- 'Awkward silence'
- 'Broken silence'
- 'Deafening silence'
- 'Suffering in silence'
- 'A minute's silence'
- 'Silence of the grave'
- 'Silent vigil'.

3 Which of these are positive, if any? Do we sometimes have a negative view of silence? If so, why? In small groups, create a story using the above expressions as key ingredients. Begin to prepare your class story by writing down one thought each. When you have finished, share your story with the rest of the class.

The Christian view

Christians experience silence not as a powerless state but as a doorway to greater understanding about themselves and their relationship with the **Divine**. They look to the example of Jesus who went away to the desert 'to be tempted by the devil for forty days and forty nights' (Matthew 4: 1–2).

Since the seventeenth century, the Quakers (the Religious Society of Friends) have used silence at the heart of their worship. Quakers call this practice 'expectant waiting', and it is about being open and letting go of thoughts. Silence is **empowering** (to empower is to give power). A **secular** example occurs in the theatre or the cinema when the lights dim and the play or film is about to start. Everyone quietens down and sits in excited anticipation of the drama to come. Thoughts and conversations are suspended as everyone waits.

In the Book of Psalms (46: 10) it says: 'Be still and know that I am God.'

Quakers believe that silence frees the individual from influences other than from God and helps a person see themselves much more clearly. *No moment of silence is a waste of time.* Silence allows people to see the uniqueness of each individual as part of God's creation. Quakers hold no **dogma** and have no **clergy** since they believe that no words or human authority can ever be powerful enough to describe their own personal relationship with God.

Did you know?

The US Navy has been testing sonar sound to detect enemy submarines. The sound is so powerful that it can kill and maim whales, dolphins and sea life. Scientists fear that with the growing number of other types of human noise in the sea (for example, oil drilling) essential biological functions – mating, feeding, navigating, nursing and communication (the ability to hear and the need to be heard) – will be destroyed.

Activity

Further activity

1 Sit comfortably for one minute in silence. Do you agree with Quakers that our minds are full of noise?

2 There are other religions that value silence. Can you discover which ones they are? Can you find out how one of them uses silence?

3 In Holland, local authorities can designate certain areas as a 'silent zone'. Imagine you are a local politician in your community. Choose which public area you would make a 'silent zone'. Write a letter to a local paper explaining your choices and what you would like to see in your 'silent zone', for example trees, benches, lighting?

Key Words

Clergy – *Priests and religious leaders in Christianity.*

Divine – *God-like.*

Dogma – *A specific set of beliefs (or doctrine) particularly when held rigidly or unquestioningly.*

Empowering – *Receiving something that gives us power.*

Secular – *Not connected with or controlled by religion.*

Solitary confinement – *To be put in a cell on your own with no contact with others.*

Thought diary

Have you had any new thoughts about the power of silence? In what ways could silence be used to improve everyday life?

Assessment

'Human greatness lies in our power of thought'
Philosopher Blaise Pascal (1623–62)

In this chapter we have explored different types of power and who, and/or what, has power.

After studying this chapter on power, do you agree with the caption above? Can you apply Pascal's thought to any of the questions below?

Here are a few questions that you might have thought about in each unit:

1. *Power play – Who or what is the boss?*
2. *An Aboriginal view – Are the elements here to heal or hurt us?*
3. *If God is all-powerful and all-loving, why is there evil in the world?*
4. *A Jewish view – Man – friend or foe?*
5. *A Hindu view – What is the relationship between the power of the body and the power of the mind?*
6. *A Christian view – Can silence give us power?*

Reflecting on your progress

1. *To help you reflect on what you have learned from this chapter, look back on your work, or in your Thought diary, and write a few lines on each of the following areas, giving reasons to improve your answers:*
   a. What I enjoyed. Why?
   b. What I found difficult. Why?

2. *Pick an idea that you liked and try to explain it clearly to another person. Think about:*
   - Where the idea came from.
   - What the idea is about.
   - Why you like the idea.
   - The *best* way to explain it to someone else.

3. *In your Thought diary, copy down five* ***skills*** *that you have used most during this chapter from the following list:*
   - I listened to others well.
   - I gave reasons for my views.
   - I expressed my ideas clearly.
   - I tried to imagine other people's point of view.
   - I developed my writing or artistic skills.
   - I investigated a new topic well.
   - I made new ideas for myself.
   - I kept on task well.
   - I used lots of imagination.
   - I cared about the feelings of other people.

4. *What facts did you learn? What do you understand now that you did not know about before? Make a spider diagram or poster to show your thoughts.*

Test yourself

1. *Why do you think silence is important for religious people? [Level 5 – AT2]*

2. *What did Martin Luther King mean when he said: 'We have guided missiles and misguided men'? Think of examples that support this statement and examples that challenge this statement. [Level 6 – AT2]*

3. *How do Jewish attitudes to the environment relate to the teachings in the Tenakh? What is the relationship between power and responsibility? [Level 7 – AT2]*

4. *What power do the elements have? Consider Aboriginal views and beliefs. [Level 8 – AT2]*

Where next?

1. *Look at the list of skills on this page. Choose three that you want to improve on in the future. Perhaps you could note them down in your Thought diary. (How could you improve them? Is there someone who could give you suggestions? Is there some way of reminding yourself?)*

2. *Think about the topic you enjoyed most. What could you do to investigate it further? Are there any websites or books that could help you find out more?*

Well done!

You know more, have thought more and have improved your skills. KEEP GOING!

Awesome!

This chapter will help you to wonder about 'space' and think about its meanings and its mysteries, by focusing on Hinduism, Buddhism, Judaism, Islam and Christianity.

When you go outside in the country on a clear, dark, silent night and look up, you will see a milky, misty-looking band stretching across the sky. You are looking into the deepest parts of the Milky Way; an enormous collection of hundreds of billions of stars, but only a small part of the universe. Do we feel that we belong in all this? Who are we? Are we just tiny insignificant dots in all this vastness? Have our lives got any meaning?

A photograph of stars being born.

Activity

Outer space

Astronomical! There are an estimated hundred billion galaxies (100,000,000,000), each with on average one hundred billion stars (100,000,000,000).

> *In the face of such overpowering numbers, what is the likelihood that only one ordinary star is accompanied by an inhabited planet? Why should we, tucked away in some forgotten corner of the cosmos, be so fortunate? To me it seems far more likely that the universe is brimming with life. But we humans do not yet know.*
>
> Carl Sagan, astronomer, 1934–96.

1. Jot down a list of other things humans 'do not yet know' (for example, the exact number of stars in the universe).
2. Write down three words to describe your thoughts/feelings about the following facts:

   A beam of light from a star travels 186,000 miles every second. The distance a beam of light travels in a year is called a **light year**. A light year measures not time but distances – enormous distances. To give you an idea of how big space is, here is how long it takes light to reach us from:

   - The Sun = eight minutes
   - The nearest star = four years
   - The centre of the Milky Way = 27,000 years!
3. Write your address so that a postman anywhere in space could find you. Now try to write the longest postal address of a bacteria living in your throat. Jot down some thoughts to the question: 'Have I a place in space?'
4. Imagine humans were able to contact intelligent life in the universe. You have been selected as an 'Earth **Envoy**'. Make a speech about what you would like other life forms to know about Earth and her inhabitants.

The Ray of Creation

The whole **cosmos** can be compared to a musical octave. Just as there are higher and lower notes in music, the whole of the cosmos has higher and lower levels. The Earth is at a higher level than the Moon and the Sun is at a higher level than the Earth. Just as your little finger is a part of your hand, your hand is a part of your arm, and so on.

The Ray of Creation

Cosmos (All) **DO**
All possible galaxies **TI**
Our Galaxy **LA**
Our Solar System **SOL**
The Sun **FA**
The Earth **MI**
The Moon **RE**
Absolute nothing **DO**

Key Words

Astronomical – *A very large amount or number.*

Cosmos – *The whole universe as an ordered whole. All that is or ever was or ever will be.*

Envoy – *A messenger sent to represent a group or a government.*

Hierarchy – *The organization of a system into higher and lower levels and energies.*

Light year – *A unit of length measuring the distance light travels in a year.*

Activity

Further activity

A place in space

1 On a large piece of paper, draw a small sketch of yourself in the middle of the page. Now try to draw four levels above you, for example, family/species, and four below you, for example, bacteria. Think of two statements that you could make about your results. What do they suggest about you and your relationship with other levels?

2 **a** Now draw a small sketch of yourself in the middle of a page and put the following in a **hierarchy** from the most important down to the least: eating, thinking, feeling, dreaming, sleeping, breathing, breeding, excreting, crying, laughing, talking, listening.

b What does your diagram suggest about you and your relationship with other levels? Is there a hierarchy like the cosmos within you? Are you a mini cosmos? Jot down any ideas you have.

3 Consider these questions:

a Scientists have discovered that the carbon that makes up our bodies was formed in the centre of stars like our sun. Do we come *into* this world or do we come *out* of it?

b The structure of an atom mirrors the structure of a solar system in that every atom is mostly empty space. If one of the atoms in your body is like a tiny solar system, what does that make you?

Thought diary

Is a thought at a much higher level than a potato? Remember that without potatoes and other foods we would soon stop thinking!

The cosmic dance

Pick out any one of these questions, and, in rough, note down any thoughts you have or answers that come to mind.

- Has space always existed or did it have a beginning?
- Does space ever change or has it always been the same?
- If space has a beginning, has it got an end?
- Is space governed by cycles of birth and death?
- Did everything happen by chance?

In this unit you will explore these questions by looking at scientific and Hindu ideas.

The Big Bang

Modern science tells us that in a great flash and fireball the universe flared forth between ten and fifteen billion years ago. This is known as the **Big Bang**, when energy blazed with an unimaginable power. The universe billowed out in every direction. However, some scientists think this expansion of the universe is slowing down and eventually will stop and reverse itself, disappearing back into a single point. Galaxies, stars and planets are born, live and die.

Activity

1 How do *you* think the universe began? Illustrate your thoughts with a drawing or painting.

2 Illustrate a cycle occurring in the world around you, for example, seasons.

3 Have a guess! When do you think that people discovered the age of the universe:

- 50 years ago?
- 100 years ago?
- 1,500 years ago?
- 3,000 years ago?
- We still do not know?

The cosmic dance

Many Hindu sacred scriptures, written around 3,000 years ago, are dedicated to explaining the origin of the universe. Hindus believe that in the life of the universe there are three forces are at work. These forces create, preserve and destroy and are represented by **Brahma**, the creator; **Vishnu**, the preserver and protector; and **Shiva**, the destroyer.

Activity

Further activity

Consider these Hindu theories carefully:

- A day in the life of Brahma, the creator god, is 8.64 billion human earth years. The lifetime of Brahma is a massive 311,040,000,000,000 earth years.
- Brahma lives as long as the universe, but each universe lasts only as long as *one* outbreath of Vishnu.
- The life of the universe is therefore like the 'out breath' of Vishnu.
- Vishnu will, in time, breath out again thus creating a new universe.
- The universe is destroyed when Vishnu begins to breathe in; Hindus consider that there is no final end to the material world, as one universe is destroyed another is created.
- In the course of the out breath of Vishnu, the galaxies and solar systems are involved in a dance of creation, preservation and destruction.
- Many Hindus believe that there are infinite numbers of universes, not just our own, endlessly coming into existence, expanding, and withdrawing in an endless cycle of death and rebirth.

1 Jot down some Hindu theories and any similarities between them and the Big Bang theory?

2 How might Hindu ideas about the universe affect the way a Hindu thinks and feels about life and death?

3 Research activity: Are modern scientists the first people to investigate space? If not, which other peoples can you think of who have? Find out more about civilizations that have worshipped ancient Sun gods, had astronomical observations, and built temples with links to the stars.

Lord of the dance. Shiva in his cosmic dance holds a drum in the upper right hand – the sound of creation. In the upper left hand is a tongue of flame, a reminder that the universe, now newly created, will, billions of years from now, be utterly destroyed.

Thought diary

Consider this:

The Big Bang is not the creation of the Cosmos but merely the end of the previous cycle.

Carl Sagan, astronomer, 1934–96.

Key Words

Big Bang – *A modern scientific theory about the origin of the universe.*

Brahma – *The Hindu deity with responsibility for creation.*

Shiva – *The Hindu deity presiding over destruction.*

Vishnu – *The Hindu deity with responsibility for preservation.*

Inner space – the final frontier?

We often take for granted the experience of life within us, our inner space.

We forget how complicated we are.

We have thoughts – worries, daydreams, concerns.

We have sensations of physical pain and pleasure.

We have feelings of love, fear, anger, joy.

Do we choose these experiences, or do they just happen automatically?

Through our senses we see only a tiny part of the world outside us – we cannot see how far away a star is.

We accept what we learn from the work of scientists.

We learn from them about the vastness of space containing strange and unexplained objects.

The space within each of us is just as strange and unexplored.

In this unit we will explore one view of inner space by looking at Buddhist beliefs.

A painting by Jon Lumberg. What do you think the artist is trying to communicate about inner and/or outer 'space'?

Activity

1 What ideas do you think the painting by Lumberg is trying to communicate?

2 Shut your eyes for one minute. Do you see anything? Do you feel anything? Do you think anything? Now jot down some thoughts about your experience. Compare them with a friend.

3 One way of exploring your inner space is to use your imagination. Imagine that your feelings are colours and your thoughts are sounds.

   a Using colours, express a positive feeling and a negative feeling you sometimes have.

   b Now make up one sound to express a negative thought and one sound to express a positive thought.

4 Scientists use telescopes, spacecraft, mathematics and many other tools to investigate outer space. What tools could we use to investigate our inner space?

The Buddhist view

Buddhists believe that it is important for us to understand our inner space. The tool they use to explore inner space is **meditation**. The purpose of meditation is to make the mind calm and peaceful.

Buddhists believe that if the mind is calm we shall be free from worries and concerns. The outer world has less effect on us and so we shall experience true happiness. However, if the mind is not peaceful, we shall find it very difficult to be happy, even if we are living in the very best conditions.

Buddhism teaches that our inner space – in other words, our attitudes and mental states – affects the way we see the world. Our attitudes and mental states will also affect us physically and emotionally. For example, if we are negative our bodies will be tense and we may feel depressed.

Through meditation Buddhists aim to clear the mind of negative thoughts and emotions. This will lead to a state of inner peace.

Buddhists consider that peace is always there within us. Like space, we do not have to make the space empty. We simply get rid of the clouds. When the clouds disappear, the nature of space is spacious, empty and limitless. When there is no cloud, the nature of the Sun and Moon reflects and shines on the Earth.

Buddhism explains that our normal state of mind is such that our thoughts and emotions are wild and unruly. As a result they control us. Mediation allows you to have some degree of control over your thoughts and emotions.

The Dalai Lama, *Transforming the mind*

Activity

Further activity

1 In the text opposite what do you think the 'clouds' represent in your inner space? (Think about thoughts or feelings that stop you feeling happy or contented.)

2 Explain, in your own words, some of the reasons why Buddhists think that meditation is important.

3 Try to jot down answers to these questions:
- Do we *decide* to think every thought we have or do they just appear from nowhere?
- Do we *decide* to feel sad or happy or does it just happen?
- Do our thoughts and emotions affect the way we see the world?

4 A **poll** in America in 2002 concluded that: 'If the focus of the twentieth century has been on outer space, the focus of the twenty-first century may well be on inner space.' Do you think this statement is true? Give reasons for your answer. Why do *you* think it is important to think about our inner space? Can you think of ways that Buddhist ideas could be used to make our everyday lives better?

Key Words

Meditation – *To calm the mind, the emotions and the body by sitting quietly.*

Poll – *Questioning a number of people to find out the general opinion about something.*

Thought diary

The average person uses less than eight per cent of their brain. If we spent more time discovering our own inner space, might our experience of the world be different?

Inner space – dreams

Dreams are a very private and powerful part of our inner space. They can often be more gripping and terrifying than our 'waking' life. They can also appear crazy, chaotic and confusing. Strange things happen that go against the natural laws of the world, for example, the law of gravity. Often dreams seem to make no sense. Can you think of some crazy or strange things that have happened in your own dream space? In this unit we will consider what you, and others, think about dreams.

Activity

1 Think of something crazy or strange that has happened in your dream space, for example, your best friend turns into an Alsatian and starts flying; or people who you would not normally meet in life are all in the same dream together. Write your dream down. If you want to you can tell it to your neighbour.

2 Working with your neighbour make a list of:

a happy elements, and

b frightening elements in any of your dreams.

Compare your findings with the rest of the class. Can you find any common elements in your dreams?

3 Pick out any two of the following questions that you are curious about and, in rough, note down any ideas or answers that come to mind:

- Can you control your dreams?
- Have you had dreams that repeat themselves?
- When you dream are you experiencing your memories?
- Are dreams just a jumble of meaningless images?
- Where do dreams come from?
- Are some dreams more important than others?
- Can you choose your dreams?

Make sure that you keep your ideas in a safe place.

A painting by Salvador Dali called 'Dream caused by the flight of a bee around a **pomegranate**, one second before awakening'.

Dreamers and interpreters

Dreams appear to have a life of their own. They are beyond our control. Many people however, believe that dreams have meaning and tell us things about our lives. A brilliant twentieth century Swiss **psychologist** called **Carl Gustav Jung** spent his life studying and **interpreting** dreams, especially his own dreams and those of his patients. He came to the conclusion that dreams can come from a very deep place within us, revealing truths about ourselves. Jung studied the dreams described in the Tenakh, the Jewish Bible, especially in the dreams of Joseph, a 17-year-old shepherd boy. Joseph, much like Jung, was an interpreter of other people's dreams as well as his own. He felt that God had given him the power to interpret dreams.

Activity

Further activity

1 Read the following three dreams of Joseph carefully:

> *Behold, we were binding sheaves in the field, and lo, my sheaf arose and stood upright; and behold your [his brothers'] sheaves gathered around it and bowed down to my sheaf.*
>
> *There were three cake baskets on my head, and in the upper most basket there were all sorts of baked foods for* ***Pharaoh****, but the birds were eating it out of the basket on my head.*
>
> *Behold, in my dream I was standing on the banks of the Nile; and seven cows, fat and sleek, came out of the Nile and fed in the reed grass; and seven other cows ate up the first seven fat cows.*
>
> Genesis 37: 8; 37: 9; 40: 16–17; 41: 17

How would you interpret these dreams? (Hint: Do the objects/animals represent anything?) Do some research: read the story in Genesis 37, 40 and 41, and find out how Joseph interpreted these dreams. Are there similarities between your interpretations and Joseph's?

2 Now read one of Carl Gustav Jung's own dreams and try to interpret it:

> *It seemed to me that I was high up in space. Far below I saw the globe of the earth, bathed in a gloriously blue light. I saw the deep blue sea and the continents. The sight of the earth from this height was the most glorious thing I had ever seen…*
>
> *Something new entered my field of vision. A short distance away I saw in space a tremendous dark block of stone, like a meteorite. It was about the size of my house, or even bigger. It was floating in space and I myself was floating in space…*
>
> *An entrance led into a small chamber. To the right of the entrance, a black Hindu sat silently in* ***lotus posture*** *upon a stone bench… I knew that he expected me.*

3 Study the dreamscape by the artist Salvador Dali carefully. Do you think it means anything? Could you interpret it?

4 Make a drawing/sketch of one of Joseph's or Jung's dreams.

5 Make a drawing/sketch of a dream that has made an impression on you.

Key Words

Carl Gustav Jung (1875–1961) – *Swiss psychologist who made breakthroughs in understanding dreams.*

Interpret – *To give a specific meaning to something.*

Lotus posture – *A position taken by Hindus to meditate. The lotus flower is a beautiful flower that grows out of mud beneath the water.*

Pharaoh – *Hebrew word for Egyptian king.*

Pomegranate – *Thick-skinned reddish fruit containing a mass of seeds.*

Psychologist – *A person who studies people's behaviour, character and the way the human mind works.*

Thought diary

We easily forget our dreams. If we write them down as soon as we wake up, we are more likely to remember them. Keep a notebook and pencil by your bed. Begin a Dream diary and record your dreams. Write down any memories you have of feelings, people, places and objects in your dreams.

Sacred space

What is your favourite space? Think of a place that makes you feel different from the normal way you feel. Jot down some thoughts about how it makes you feel. Is this place special for other people as well?

In this unit we will look at the way certain spaces are regarded as **sacred** spaces by learning from the Muslim tradition.

Activity

1 Wish you were here! A sacred space is a very special space that helps and refreshes a person's mind, body, and spirit. Think of somewhere in the world that is a sacred space for you. It does not have to be religious, but a place that helps and refreshes you. Imagine you are there. Write a postcard to your friend describing this space and how you feel about it.

2 Many buildings in the modern world are designed for function not feeling: multi-storey car parks, tower blocks and supermarkets, for example. Is part of the function of a space to help people feel refreshed? Design a space in your school that will refresh, relax and revive people. Where would it be? What would be in it (for example, bells, incense, music, beanbags)? What would happen in it? What rules would there be (for example, would eating/shouting/mobile phones be allowed?)

3 Is the space around you different from any other space? How do you feel when somebody gets close to 'your space'? Invaded? Irritable? Insecure? Inviting? Try it with a friend. Face each other about five metres away. Ask your friend to take one step slowly towards you then stop. How do you feel? Your friend takes another step. How do you feel? And so on. Write down a few words or a short poem about your feelings.

Sacred space: Makkah

Makkah is located in the mountains of Saudi Arabia. It is the centre of the Islamic world. It is also the birthplace of the Prophet Muhammad (pbuh) (570–632 AD).

The city contains the most sacred space in Islam, the **Ka'bah**. The Ka'bah, a cube-shaped building, was built by the **Prophet Abraham** over 3,000 years ago, with direct instructions from God about its dimensions and location.

It was the first **sanctuary** on Earth dedicated to the worship of One God. The structure's corners are in line with the compass points, north, south, east and west. Inside is an empty room with a marble floor and three wooden pillars supporting the roof. The Ka'bah is draped with a woven black silk covering with verses from the Qur'an embroidered in gold. In one corner of the Ka'bah is the Black Stone, said to be a meteorite.

The Ka'bah is known as the Sacred House and stands in the courtyard of the Sacred Mosque. Ringed by seven towering minarets and 64 gates, this magnificent building is capable of holding more than 1.2 million pilgrims at the same time.

Two million Muslims perform the **Hajj** (**pilgrimage** to Makkah) each year. The Hajj pilgrimage is the fifth of the Muslim practices known as the **five pillars of Islam**, and must be performed at least once in a lifetime by all adults, health and finances permitting. When pilgrims are about ten kilometres from Makkah, they wrap two white seamless sheets around the body to indicate the equality and purity of the pilgrim.

Activity

Further activity

1 Read the paragraphs about Makkah and reflect on what they say about Islam and sacred space. How might a pilgrimage to Makkah help and refresh Muslims? Imagine you were visiting Makkah on the Hajj. Write a postcard home describing your experiences.

2 Muslims pray five times a day, and in a sense Makkah is visited by all Muslims every day. Whenever Muslims pray, alone or together, they face towards Makkah. This focus and direction of prayer is called the **qibla**. Is there somewhere you have a special connection with? Do you do something, or display some symbol, or have a souvenir of your connection to this place?

What does this photograph of the Ka'bah tell you about sacred space?

Key Words

Five pillars of Islam – *Five duties for all Muslims.*

Hajj – *Pilgrimage to Makkah, the fifth pillar of Islam.*

Ka'bah – *The most sacred space in Islam.*

Pilgrimage – *A journey to a sacred place.*

Prophet Abraham – *A major prophet of the One God.*

Qibla – *The direction Muslims turn in prayer towards the Ka'bah.*

Sacred – *Something that is holy.*

Sanctuary – *Part of a sacred space that is considered most holy.*

Thought diary

Choose either

a a place where you have felt happy and really at home in, or

b a famous sacred building or place, for example, the Pyramids.

Make a study of it. Gather pictures, photographs and stories about it. Write a poem.

Try to make the reader 'feel' this place.

Running out of space?

Two billion people alive today are under 15 years old. You are one of the largest-ever generations living on the planet at any one time! It took thousands of years for the world to reach one billion people (which it did in 1804). By 1960, the world's population had increased to three billion and on 12 October 1999 it reached six billion.

Your generation will have to consider whether natural resources and food will run out, whether there will be enough space to get away from the crowds, or whether overpopulation will lead to the destruction of the human race. The answers to these questions may affect your life and your decisions about having your own children.

So are we running out of space? All the world religions have something to say about questions like these contemporary moral issues. In this unit you will look at the view of the Roman Catholic Church that the real issue is not overpopulation, but how we distribute the world's resources.

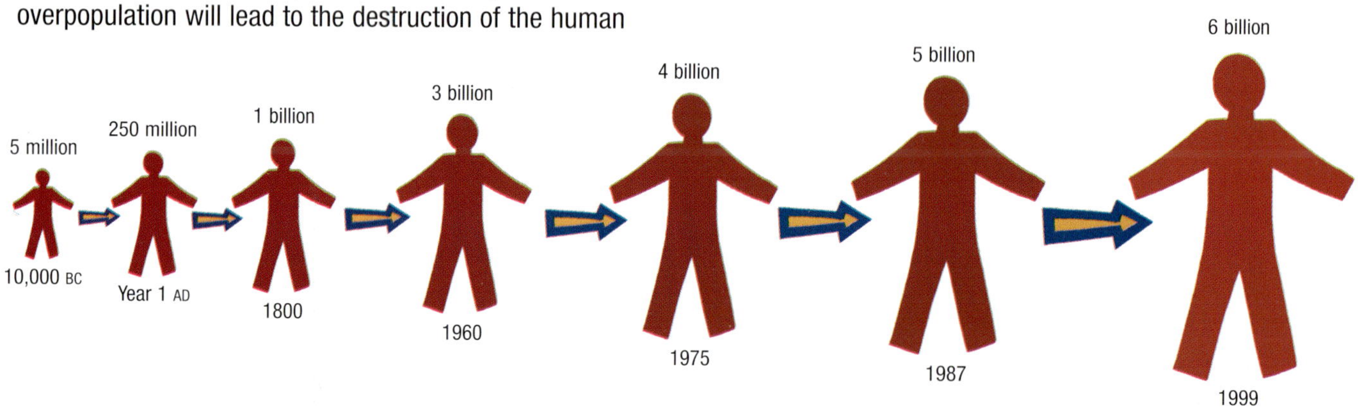

The population of India and China is now equal to the world population of 1975.

Activity

1 Every second five people are born and two people die, a net gain of three people per second. At this rate, the world population is doubling every 40 years. When you are 50, the population could be double what it is now. By the time you are 80, it could have doubled again. And by 2120, it will be 48 billion. Eight times more people for the same amount of space! Design a diagram or picture illustrating these or any other statistics in this unit.

2 In pairs, brainstorm some of the problems caused by overpopulation. Then brainstorm solutions to these problems. Record your findings.

3 Imagine you are head of a mission beginning a new **colony** in space. You have to think up plans and rules for the future of your colony. Write a report on what you would do about population growth.

The Roman Catholic view

Some parts of the world, like India, China and South America, have experienced population 'explosions'. Some people argue that the solution is to promote **birth control** – but is this the answer?

The Roman Catholic Church teaches that sex has a natural purpose, that is, the reproduction of the species. The use of **contraceptives** (the condom, for example) is 'unnatural' because it interferes with this natural process. Many Catholics do not use birth control and some argue that birth control is not the answer to 'overpopulation'.

However **AIDS** –transmitted by unprotected sex – raises other questions. Can you think what they are?

Roman Catholics argue that poverty, not overpopulation, is the root cause of many of the world's problems. With two-thirds of the world's population living in poverty, the only security that people can find is in their children. Children are sent out to work to support their relatives.

The only way to reduce the birth rate is to **redistribute** the world's wealth. World hunger is not caused by overpopulation but by the fact that food is not distributed fairly. What right have people in the 'rich world' to tell the majority in the 'poor world' to stop having children?

Activity

Further activity

1 Explain in your own words the meaning of the diagram opposite.

2 • The State of Western Australia: 974,843 square miles: 1.7 million people
  • Mexico City, Mexico: 900 square miles: 22 million people

If you were a Roman Catholic priest working in Western Australia, might your opinions about birth control be different to that of a priest working in Mexico City? Give reasons for your answer.

3 The **United Nations** calls 11 July World Population Day. Design a poster/book cover highlighting what you think are the most important issues surrounding the world's population and the future.

4 Consider whether overpopulation causes poverty, or whether poverty causes overpopulation. Give reasons for your views.

Key Words

AIDS – *Acquired Immune Deficiency Syndrome. Death from AIDS is actually death from a range of infections or cancers caused by HIV (Human Immuno-deficiency Virus).*

Birth control – *To control when and how many children to have.*

Colony – *A group of people with similar backgrounds living in a far-off place.*

Contraceptives – *Methods by which pregnancy can be avoided.*

Redistribute – *To share out again in a different way.*

United Nations – *Organization of different countries working together to make the world a fairer and more peaceful place.*

Thought diary

Are we running out of space? Consider the following:

20 per cent of the world's population in the developed world use up 86 per cent of the world's resources… yet the rich world has a population growth of almost zero. Enough food could be produced to feed billions more people. A study by the World Wildlife Fund in 2002 warned that: 'If all the world's people consumed natural resources at the same rate as the average American or British citizen we would require at least two extra planets by 2050'.

Assessment

In this chapter we have explored ideas about our relationship to both outer space and inner space.

Here are a few questions that you might have thought about in each unit:

1. *Awesome – Have we any significance in space?*
2. *A Hindu view – What is space?*
3. *A Buddhist view – Is inner space the final frontier for discovery?*
4. *A Jewish view – Do dreams mean anything?*
5. *A Muslim view – What makes a space sacred?*
6. *A Roman Catholic view – Are we running out of space?*

Reflecting on your progress

1. *To help you reflect on what you have learned from this chapter, look back on your work, or in your Thought diary, and write a few lines on each of the following areas giving reasons to improve your answers:*
   - (a) What I enjoyed. Why?
   - (b) What I found difficult. Why?
2. *Pick an idea that you liked and try to explain it clearly to another person. Think about:*
   - Where the idea came from.
   - What the idea is about.
   - Why you like the idea.
   - The *best* way to explain it to someone else.
3. *In your Thought diary, copy down five* ***skills*** *that you have used most during this chapter from the following list:*
   - I listened to others well.
   - I gave reasons for my views.
   - I expressed my ideas clearly.
   - I tried to imagine other people's point of view.
   - I developed my writing or artistic skills.
   - I investigated a new topic well.
   - I made new ideas for myself.
   - I kept on task well.
   - I used lots of imagination.
   - I cared about the feelings of other people.
4. *What facts did you learn? What do you understand now that you did not know about before? Make a spider diagram or poster to show your thoughts.*

Test yourself

1. *What do you think of Hindu ideas regarding how the universe works? Give reasons for your answers [Level 5 – AT2]*
2. *How does meditation help a Buddhist explore their inner space? [Level 6 – AT2]*
3. *Does overpopulation cause poverty or does poverty cause overpopulation? How might a Roman Catholic respond to this question? [Level 7 – AT2]*
4. *What is the importance of a Muslim performing the Hajj? What events does the Hajj commemorate and why? Why do you think we have sacred spaces, and what function do you think they serve? [Level 8 – AT2]*

Where next?

Where next?

1. *Look at the list of skills on the opposite page. Choose two that you want to improve on in the future. Perhaps you could note them down in your Thought diary. (How could you improve them? Is there someone who could give you suggestions? Is there some way of reminding yourself?)*

2. *Think about the topic you enjoyed most. What could you do to investigate it further? Are there any websites or books that could help you find out more?*

Well done!

You know more, have thought more and have improved your skills.

KEEP GOING!

What is time?

This chapter will help you to wonder about 'time' and recreate your own ideas about its mysteries and importance. It will also introduce some different views about time from the religions of Hinduism, Islam, Buddhism, Christianity and Judaism.

Choose one of these questions, and, in rough, note down any ideas or answers that come to mind:

- What is time?
- Can we really 'save' it or 'spend' it like money?
- Does your past or your future exist in the present somehow?
- Is time the same in our dreams as when we are awake?
- Did time exist before the universe did?
- Will time travel be possible one day?

Many people throughout the centuries have wondered about time, and perhaps with good reason. It is something that we cannot directly see, hear, taste, feel or smell, and yet it may be more valuable to us than any object on Earth. It can tick away, fly by, or drag. It is both very mysterious, and very important. This chapter will help you to explore what you, and others, think about time.

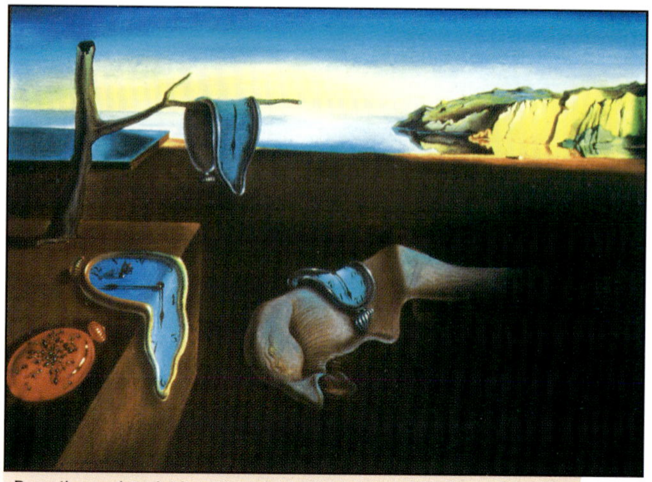

Does time only exist in our minds? Can it change?

Do you love life? Then do not squander time, for that's the stuff life is made of.

Benjamin Franklin, American scientist and politician (1706–90)

Activity

How well do we use time?

Read the song lyrics below carefully:

Pink Floyd: *Time* (Mason, Waters, Wright, Gilmour)

Ticking away the moments that make up a dull day
You fritter and waste the hours in an off-hand way
Kicking around on a piece of ground in your home town
Waiting for someone or something to show you the way. ***line 4***

Tired of lying in the sunshine staying home to watch the rain
You are young and life is long and there is time to kill today
And then one day you find ten years have got behind you
No one told you when to run, you missed the starting gun. ***line 8***

Activity

continued...

And you run and you run to catch up with the sun, but it's sinking
And racing around to come up behind you again
The sun is the same in a relative way, but you're older
Shorter of breath and one day closer to death. ***line 12***

Every year is getting shorter, never seem to find the time
Plans that come to naught or half a page of scribbled lines
Hanging on in quiet desperation is the English way
The time is gone the song is over, thought I'd something more to say. ***line 16***

Now answer the following questions with your own opinions:

1 Why do you think the songwriter says 'Every year is getting shorter' (line 13), when every year lasts an equal 365 days?

2 In the last line, the songwriter 'thought he had something more to say'. Why do you think he said that?

3 What is this song saying about time, our lives, and how we use them?

4 If you met the songwriter, what might he say to you and what would you say to him?

Activity

Further activity

Reflect on these facts, and express your thoughts about them.

If the history of all life on Earth was squashed in to a single year (a total of about 2,000,000,000 years in reality), then the following things start to exist on these dates:

- **1 January** basic organisms
- **23 September** animals with bones and muscles
- **21 November** dinosaurs
- **19 December** dinosaurs die out
- **31 December (evening)** human beings

Dinosaurs were on Earth for nearly a month (165 million years)! The last 6,000 years – from the ancient Egyptians to the modern day – would last just 90 seconds up to midnight on New Year's Eve. The average lifespan of a human would be just 1.25 seconds.

1 Is human life 'long' or 'short'? Can it be both? Explain your opinions.

2 If humans had existed from 1 January, would that change the view we have of ourselves? How and why?

3 Invent the next '90 seconds' (6,000 years). What do you think will happen to humans, the world, and to nature over this time?

Thought diary

Pick any question that has made you think differently about time or life, and write down your views about it. You could also create a picture or a collage about 'time and life'.

A friend or enemy?

Is time your friend or your enemy? Does it control you or do you control it? Investigating different ideas about time may help us to develop our own views about it. This unit will explore what Hindus think about time and how it might affect their lives.

Activity

1 In pairs, brainstorm all the phrases you can think of that include the word 'time'. (For example, 'running out of time', or 'time flies when you're having fun'.)

2 Share your ideas with other groups, and add any new ones to your list.

3 Now reflect on how we talk about time. What do the phrases suggest about how we feel or think about it? For example, what does 'time flies when you're having fun' suggest about how we notice the passing of time?

This watch, made in 1650, is inscribed with 'reminders' in Latin: 'The hour of death is uncertain', 'Life flies like an hour', 'While you live, live to live'. Why do you think someone would want such a strange object? How might it affect them?

The Hindu view

One Hindu view of time is to see it as something that must be escaped from, or 'to go beyond'. Time brings us into existence at birth, takes us through the difficulties and pains of life, and finally on to death, when we will be reborn into another life. This cycle of birth, growth, death and **rebirth** has happened to us – our souls – thousands of times before, and it will continue to happen over and over again. This is why Hindus often picture time as a wheel that our souls are bound to, turning us through lifetimes of suffering as many different living creatures.

> *Just as a person puts on new garments and gives up the old ones, so the soul accepts new bodies, giving up the old and useless ones.*
>
> Bhagavad Gita 2:22

This image may seem depressing, but there is good news too: it is possible to escape from this wheel of time and the sufferings that it can bring us. If we have been good enough to be reborn as a human, we have a very precious chance to follow religious teachings and learn how to free our souls from the clutches of time (it would be much harder as a rat or a pig). Release from the wheel is called **moksha** or 'liberation', and our souls then experience perfect and eternal happiness. No more death, or fear, or pain. Someone who has achieved this is sometimes called **kala-atita** or 'one who has gone beyond time'.

This cycle of birth, death and rebirth is also thought to happen to the whole universe as well. Each universe is said to exist for one lifetime of the creator god called **Brahma**; a massive 311,040,000,000,000 years, after which a new universe eventually begins again.

So for Hindus, time does not have a beginning or an end, but works in cycles of longer (a universe) or shorter (a human life) periods. Everything is involved in a process of 'creation, destruction, to more creation' through time. From one view then, a human life is a very precious chance to free our souls from the cycle of time. From another view though, a single lifetime is an incredibly small moment in the whole cycle of universal time; all living things have had many lives before as all sorts of living creatures, and they will go on to have many more too.

Activity

Further activity

1. In what way does this Hindu view of time differ from that of modern science and the 'Big Bang'? Try to explain an important difference in your own words.
2. Do you think that Hindus view time as an enemy or as a friend? What do you think?
3. Create a diagram that explains the Hindu view of the 'cycle of life'.
4. How do you think the Hindu belief in rebirth affects the way they relate to other creatures or feel about death?

Key Words

Brahma – *A Hindu god responsible for bringing everything into existence.*

Kala-atita – *'One who has transcended (or gone beyond) time'; someone who is perfectly at peace and happy.*

Moksha – *Liberation or freedom from the wheel of time: a state of bliss.*

Rebirth – *When the soul (or 'atman') moves from one life, through death, to the next life.*

Thought diary

Did you discover any new ideas in this unit? Make a note of them in your diary. It may help to make a diagram as well as to write about them.

Lifetimes?

In pairs, select a question that you are curious about, and jot down your first thoughts about it:

- What do you think happens after life has ended?
- Is there nothing at all, a Heaven, a Hell, or another life?
- If there is an afterlife of some sort, what part of us continues?

Different religions have varying ideas about what happens after this life. Buddhists, Sikhs and Hindus believe in reincarnation. Muslims, Jews and Christians, however, believe that there is an everlasting afterlife. This unit will help you to investigate your own, and Muslim, beliefs about afterlives.

A vision of Hell. But is Hell an actual place? What else could it be?

Activity

1 Create a survey of afterlife beliefs in your class. What do people believe will happen after life? Copy the table below to help you gather your information.

2 Now make a bar or pie chart to display the results.

3 Which was the most popular belief? Why do you think that was?

4 Which was the least popular belief? Again, suggest reasons for this.

5 Do you think it is reasonable for people to believe in an afterlife without believing in a religion? Explain your view on this.

Place a tick in the relevant row:

I think this one is most likely	Tick for each vote
Reincarnation – I will come back as another living thing	
Heaven – I will go to Heaven for eternity	
Heaven or Hell – I may go to Heaven / Hell if I am good / bad	
Nothing – there is nothing after this life	
Other possibilities (for example, I will become a ghost)	

The Muslim view

Islam teaches that this life is a brief preparation period for **akhirah** (the 'hereafter') that will last forever. When a Muslim dies, he or she will be taken by an angel to wait in comfort or in torment in a place called **barzakh**. The souls wait for the **Day of Judgement** when all life on Earth will come to an end. All the souls are then judged by Allah. Good people will go to Heaven for ever, but those who were greedy and selfish will go to Hell.

> *Truly a Day in the sight of the Lord is like a thousand years of your reckoning.*
>
> Qur'an: Surah 22: 47

But why do Muslims believe this?

One very important source of information for Muslim belief is the Qur'an, the direct word of Allah, recited to Muslims by **Muhammad (pbuh)** about 1,400 years ago. The holy book gives Muslims advice on how to live a good life so that they may go to Heaven and avoid Hell. The **Prophet** Muhammad (pbuh) was Allah's last and greatest messenger. He was said to have experienced Heaven and Hell for himself, and this occasion is remembered today as 'laylat al-Isra wa al-Mir'aj' or 'The Night Journey and Ascension'.

> *The Companions of the Right Hand in the Garden shall ask of the wretched: 'What led you into hell fire?' They will say, 'We were not of those who prayed, nor those who fed the poor, and we wasted our time away with empty arguments, and we rejected as a lie the Day of Judgement – until what is certain came upon us.'*
>
> Qur'an: Surah 74: 39–47

Activity

Further activity

1. How do you think a Muslim's belief about the afterlife affects their **a** thoughts; **b** feelings and **c** actions?
2. Why do you think Muslims believe in this afterlife?
3. Do you think there are disadvantages to having a belief in an afterlife, or is it all 'good news'?
4. Using the information above, make a flow diagram showing what may happen to a Muslim after this life. Include the journey to barzakh with the angel, the Day of Judgement, Allah's judgement, and Heaven and Hell.

Key Words

Akhirah – *The 'hereafter' or afterlife believed in by Muslims.*

Barzakh – *Meaning the 'barrier'; where souls wait for the Day of Judgement.*

Day of Judgement – *A day in the future when all living beings, past and present, are judged and go to Heaven or Hell.*

Muhammad (pbuh) – *The last and greatest prophet of Allah who lived 570–632 CE.*

Prophet – *A messenger of God; someone chosen to spread the word of God.*

Thought diary

Where do you get your beliefs about the afterlife from? A special book? Science? A person you trust? Note down any ideas this unit gave you. Try researching another religious view about afterlife.

Is time always changing me?

Marion looked puzzled:

MARION: This might sound daft, Keith, but do you think we are just our body?

KEITH: What do you mean?

MARION: Well it says in this magazine that over 80 per cent of a human being is made up of water. I mean, is that all we are? Just bones and water, with a bit of fat and gristle? There's got to be more to me than that, surely!

KEITH: Of course there is! There's a *me* inside my body, isn't there? Everyday you wake up, look in the bathroom mirror, and you say to yourself: 'It's me! There I am again!'

MARION: True! But what is that 'me'? Is it just my face and body? Have 'I' always been there since I was a baby? I mean, does it change over time?

KEITH: I'm not sure. The 'me' might be your mind, I suppose. Or maybe a soul, but I've no idea what that actually is to be honest.

MARION: Or are 'you' your memories? We need to think this out a bit…

A painting by Magritte. What do you think it suggests about 'seeing ourselves'?

Activity

1 Read the passage above again, and take time to think about it. What does it make you wonder about? What questions would you like to look into a bit more? (Are Keith and Marion mad?)

2 Share your thoughts and questions with others. In groups, try to work out what this 'me' is that people seem to feel inside themselves. Aim to create a sentence or two that will explain your views to everyone else.

The Buddhist view about 'me'

Most religions say that humans have something inside of themselves – a soul – that never changes. It is the 'me' part of us; the part that feels the feelings, thinks the thoughts and gives life to the body. It can survive death, and live on for ever. However, Buddhism claims that there is no soul or 'unchanging me' inside us at all. Why do they say this?

Buddhists believe that if we really look closely within ourselves, we will not be able to find anything that remains the same – an 'I' - over time. This idea is known as **anatta** or 'not self'. It may *seem* as though we have an unchanging someone inside that thinks and feels things, but it is only an appearance or an illusion. If you go searching for what it is that does all the thinking or feeling, you will not find it because it is not there! All you will find is simply more thoughts or feelings, and they are always changing. Buddhists often use the image of a river to explain this:

Life is just like a mountain river, flowing far and swift, taking everything along with it; there is no moment, no instant, no second when it stops flowing, but it goes on flowing and continuing.
The Pali Canon

You can never step into the same river twice.
Heraclitus, a Greek philosopher, 536–470 BCE

Activity

Further activity

1 Think of a river you know. The name of the river may stay the same (the River Thames, for example), but is the river itself ever the same in two different moments? List what changes and what might stay the same.

2 Does this give you any ideas about what changes or stays the same in a human being? Write down your thoughts.

3 Do you think that this Buddhist image for a human being is right? Is there anything about a human being that you think stays exactly the same over time? Is everything about you always changing?

4 Imagine the Buddhist view is right. How do you think it would make you feel, think and act?

Key Words

Anatta – *Meaning 'not self'; the Buddhist idea that we have no 'me' that is always the same within us.*

The Pali Canon – *A collection of Buddhist scriptures written about 2,000 years ago.*

Thought diary

What are your thoughts about the 'me' inside? Has the Buddhist view made you think about yourself differently? Jot down any thoughts or feelings that you have.

In the beginning...

When and how did life begin? Were humans made by God on the 'sixth day of creation', as the Bible claims, or did life evolve over billions of years? This unit will help you to make up your own mind about how we look at the Bible, science, and belief.

Charles Darwin's theory of evolution suggests that:	The Bible suggests that:
Life was formed over millions of years	The world was created by God in six days
Humans evolved from apes	Humans were made in 'God's image'
Life is a natural process where the 'fittest' survive	Life is given by God
Life began by chance	Life began as part of God's plan

Activity

To start with, have a class vote on which version of creation most likely to be true: **Charles Darwin**'s theory of evolution or the Bible story. Why do you think people voted in that way?

Now read the information on 'The Monkey Trial', and, in groups or as a class, create a modern version of it.

The Creation of Adam, by Michelangelo, painted 500 years ago.

The Monkey Trial

Christian fundamentalists took American schoolteacher John Scopes to court in 1925, accusing him of breaking Tennessee law by teaching Darwin's theory of evolution in his lessons. They claimed that the theory contradicted the truth of the **Creation story** in the Bible, and they particularly disagreed with the idea of 'humans descending from monkeys'.

John was defended by Clarence Darrow, a lawyer who wanted to show that the Bible could not be literally true, and that the theory of evolution made more sense. However, William Bryan was a lawyer and Christian fundamentalist who sought to find John guilty and defend the literal truth of the Bible. The Monkey Trial was broadcast on radio, and, after a week of heated arguments, John was found guilty of breaking the law. He was fined $100. To this day, some teachers in the southern states of America refuse to teach the theory of evolution.

Darwin thought that humans developed from apes.

Roles

a Judge

b Prosecutor (supporting the Bible version of creation)

c Defence (supporting the evolutionary account of creation)

d John Scopes

e A jury

f Reporters for newspapers and radio

Scene suggestions

- Darrow and Bryan make their cases.
- The jury discuss the evidence in private.
- John defends himself.
- Reporters give radio updates of any 'juicy bits' of the trial.
- The judge summarizes the trial and gives a sentence (if found guilty).

Arguments that Christians might use to defend the Creation story: (Can you use any of them in your courtroom drama?)

1. God is omnipotent (all-powerful). Creating the world in six days is therefore perfectly possible.
2. A lot of the Bible is like a poem. It tells us things in images, but it should not be taken literally (word for word) all the time.
3. Fossils were put on Earth by the Devil to challenge our belief in the truth of the Bible.
4. Science and religion are just two different ways of looking at life. They do not clash.
5. The theory of evolution is just a theory. No one can say that it is definitely true. Someone will probably invent another theory in 100 years time.
6. People did not know any better when the Bible was written (they also thought that the Earth was flat!). The theory of evolution just explains the mystery a little more. It does not mean that God does not exist or that the Bible is telling lies.

What arguments might be used against these Christian views?

Did you know?

There are many different sorts of Christians, and they interpret the Bible in different ways. Many fundamentalist Christians think that the words in the Bible are literally true, but others interpret it more like a poem.

Activity

Further activity

Carry out a survey on how people view the Creation story in the Bible. Who believes that it is false? Who thinks it is true in a poetic way? Who thinks that it is literally true? Gather some results, and see if you can summarize them in a few sentences. Have people's views changed since the class vote at the beginning? Why or why not?

Key Words

Charles Darwin (1809–82) – *Scientist who published* The Origin of Species *in 1859, and introduced the theory of evolution.*

Christian fundamentalists – *Christians who have a literal or strict way of interpreting the Bible 'word for word'.*

Creation story – *The Biblical story (in Genesis) of how everything was created by God.*

Thought diary

Have your views changed about anything? What did you find interesting in this unit? Jot down your own ideas or feelings in your diary.

Times of your life!

What have been, or will be, the most important times of your life? Think, for example, of ceremonies that you may have been to that have marked the times of someone's birth, marriage, or death. These occasions are called **rites of passage** because they mark the start of a passage or important change in people's lives.

One rite of passage that many cultures celebrate is when a 'child' becomes an 'adult'. But what do you think an 'adult' is, and when exactly does a child become one? Is it when:

- you can drive a car?
- you get married?
- you are eighteen years old?
- you first have a job?
- you are capable of having children?
- you pass some kind of special 'adulthood' test?

...or some other reason? This unit will help you explore what you think about 'being an adult' by looking at how Jews mark this occasion.

Activity

Read about **Bar** and **Bat Mitzvah** below. Create a flow chart (with diagrams and words) of what a young Jew will do during this rite of passage.

A Jewish girl becomes an adult at the age of 12 in a ceremony called Bat Mitzvah. It means 'daughter of the **commandments**', suggesting that she is ready to take responsibility for her own actions, and particularly her own religious life. A Jewish boy becomes an adult at 13. The ceremony is called Bar Mitzvah, meaning 'son of the commandments'. These ages are also recognized as the start of **puberty**. Both boys and girls will prepare for the ceremony weeks or months in advance and it has three main sections to it:

1 The child will read from the Torah (Jewish holy scriptures) in the language of Hebrew. This takes place in the **synagogue**, where friends and relatives have gathered to witness this special occasion.

2 The father of the child then gives a speech, thanking God for bringing their child to maturity, and declaring that the child is now an adult, responsible for their own actions in life. Often the **rabbi** will also give a speech, congratulating the child and encouraging them to follow the teachings of Judaism.

3 This is followed by a celebration involving a meal, the giving of gifts (especially religious books), and a short speech of thanks given by the new adult to his parents in front of friends and family.

So, 'becoming an adult' for a Jewish person means:

a being responsible for your actions and your own religious life;

b confirming your identity as a Jew;

c thanking those who have helped you through childhood to adulthood.

This young Jewish person becomes an adult in a special rite of passage

Research challenge! Can you find out what special items a Jew wears in a synagogue, and why they wear them?

Activity

Further activity

1 How do you think a young Jew feels at the Bar or Bat Mitzvah ceremony? (List three feelings.)

2 Working individually or in pairs, invent your own 'rite of passage' to celebrate becoming an adult. You might want to think about these questions:

- **a** How old would you be? Why then?
- **b** Where would you have the rite?
- **c** Who would be there?
- **d** Would there be any speeches? By who, and saying what?
- **e** Would there be special music, food, gifts or clothes?
- **f** How could other people recognize the moment when you change from being a 'child' to an 'adult'?
- **g** Would there be a 'test of adulthood' before the rite? If so, what would it be?

3 Create a display or presentation with pictures, diagrams, writing, and perhaps music to express your ideas for others to appreciate.

Key Words

Bar/Bat Mitzvah – *Meaning son/daughter of the commandments. The ceremony when a Jewish girl or boy officially becomes an adult.*

Commandments – *God-given rules for Jews to follow.*

Puberty – *When a person becomes biologically able to have children.*

Rabbi – *Religious teacher and leader of a Jewish community.*

Rite of passage – *A ceremony (rite) that marks a significant time in a person's life.*

Synagogue – *Jewish place of worship.*

Thought diary

How would you define what an adult is now? Try to explain it in just three or four sentences: 'An adult is someone who…' Say whether you will actually use your rite of passage when you become an adult.

Is this a good way to mark the special time when you become an adult?

Assessment

In this chapter we have begun to think about time and how it might affect our lives in different ways.

What do you think about 'time' now?
What ideas does this picture suggest to you?

Have your thoughts about time changed since you started to think about it? Try to explain how.

Here are a few questions that you might have thought about in each unit:

1. *About time – How do we use our 'life time'?*
2. *A Hindu view – Is time our friend or enemy?*
3. *A Muslim view – What happens after this life?*
4. *A Buddhist view – Does anything about me **not** change?*
5. *A Christian view – Are we the product of time or God?*
6. *A Jewish view – How should we measure the 'times of our lives'?*

Reflecting on your progress

1. *To help you reflect on what you have learned from this chapter, look back on your work, or in your Thought diary, and write a few lines on each of the following areas, giving reasons to improve your answers:*
   a. What I enjoyed. Why?
   b. What I found difficult. Why?
2. *Pick an idea that you liked and try to explain it clearly to another person. Think about:*
   - Where the idea came from.
   - What the idea is about.
   - Why you like the idea.
   - The *best* way to explain it to someone else.
3. *In your Thought diary, copy down five **skills** that you have used most during this chapter from the following list:*
   - I listened to others well.
   - I gave reasons for my views.
   - I expressed my ideas clearly.
   - I tried to imagine other people's point of view.

- I developed my writing or artistic skills.
- I investigated a new topic well.
- I made new ideas for myself.
- I kept on task well.
- I used lots of imagination.
- I cared about the feelings of other people.

4. *What facts did you learn? What do you understand now that you did not know about before? Make a spider diagram or poster to show your thoughts.*

Test yourself

1. *Why do you think it is important for people to think about how they use their lifetime? See if you can find an example in this chapter to help you answer the question. [Level 5 – AT2]*
2. *The Buddha's last words were: 'All things will decay, so be mindful and work hard at finding true happiness.' Do you think this attitude is depressing, realistic or positive about life? Support your choice with examples or ideas [Level 6 – AT2]*
3. *'Getting drunk on your eighteenth birthday is the only way to celebrate becoming an adult!' How might a Jew respond to this comment? Do you agree with their view? Remember to give reasons for your answers. [Level 7 – AT2]*
4. *Has the scientific theory of evolution proved that the Bible is just a fairytale? Try to give several points of view in your answer. [Level 8 – AT2]*

Where next?

1. *Look at the list of skills above. Choose three that you want to improve on in the future. Perhaps you could note them down in your Thought diary. (How could you improve them? Is there someone who could give you suggestions? Is there some way of reminding yourself?)*
2. *Think about the topic you enjoyed most. What could you do to investigate it further? Are there any websites or books that could help you find out more?*
3. *Try to find out what Sikhs think about 'afterlife'. Try using the web or a book from your library. (Try www.sikhs.org or www.allaboutsikhs.com.)*

Well done!

You know more, have thought more and have improved your skills.

KEEP GOING!

The breakdown

This chapter will explore communication by looking at Hinduism, Islam, Sikhism, Buddhism and Judaism.

Pick out one of these questions and, in rough, note down any ideas or answers that come to mind:

- What would the world be like if there was no communication?
- What happens if people do not communicate?
- Does it matter if people do not communicate?

Activity

1 Since you got up this morning you have communicated with others and others have communicated with you. List the ways you and others have communicated (for example, speaking to your sister or brother over breakfast).

2 Imagine you woke up this morning in an unknown house surrounded by an unknown family. Look at your list again. Would the way you communicate change? Might communication not have happened in this new situation? Jot down your answers.

3 Imagine this family are from a different country to you with a different culture. Would there be communication problems? Could communication be made harder by expecting *not* to understand each other? What important 'key thoughts' could you keep in mind to aid communication (for example, watch your **body language**). Make a list of your 'key thoughts'. Keep a record of them.

Breakdown in communication

Although human beings have created amazing **communications technologies** (for example, the Internet, mobile phones and satellites), it seems that they still cannot communicate effectively. Every day in the **media** there are examples of conflict. War and **sectarian** violence (for example, in Northern Ireland) are the ultimate breakdowns in communication. Enemies sometimes claim that the root of their conflicts with each other is religion. But is it religion or human error and misunderstandings that inspire violence?

Activity

Further activity

- A site at Ayodhya in Northern India is holy to both Hindus and Muslims.
- A Muslim emperor built a mosque at the site in 1528 CE. Hindus claim that the site had a Hindu temple there for hundreds of years before this.
- The British, who ruled India in the nineteenth century, took control of the mosque in 1859 and made separate worship areas for Hindus and Muslims.
- In 1992, Hindus tore down the mosque with sledgehammers, crow-bars and their bare hands.
- Over 3,000 Muslims and hundreds of Hindus died in the riots that followed.
- In the twenty first century some Hindus are planning to build a new Hindu temple on the site.
- Hindus returning on a train from the site were fire-bombed by Muslim mobs, burning 60 Hindus to death.
- In revenge, mobs of Hindus killed hundreds of Muslim men, women and children.

1 Imagine you are a Special Peace **Envoy** to India and your job is to bring peace to the region. Consider your earlier 'key thoughts' about communication very carefully and apply them to this situation. What would you do to encourage communication and mutual understanding?

2 As a Peace Envoy to India you are given two documents to read and study:

Document 1: Islam

If one knows the true meaning of Islam, there will be no wars. All that will be heard are the sounds of prayer and the greetings of peace. Only the resonance of God will be heard. That is the ocean of Islam. That is unity. That is our wealth and our true weapon. Not the sword in your hand.

Sufi Shaikh M.R. Bawa Muhaiyaddeen quoted in *Testing the Global Ethic*

Activity

Further activity continued...

Document 2: Hinduism

Literally speaking, ***ahimsa*** *means 'non-killing'. But to me it has a world of meaning, and it takes me into realms much higher, infinitely higher. It really means that you may not harbour an uncharitable thought, even in connection with one who may consider himself to be your enemy.*

Mahatma Gandhi

3 Using some of the ideas in these documents, write a report about the situation for a newspaper read by both Hindus and Muslims. Make sure you address:

- **a** where you think communication has broken down;
- **b** why you think communication has broken down;
- **c** how you think lines of communication could be restored.

What, if anything, is this man communicating?

Key Words

Ahimsa – *The Indian principle of avoiding harm to any living creature in thought or deed.*

Body language – *Communicating through body postures.*

Communication technologies – *Technology – including the Internet, mobile phones and satellites – that carries information.*

Envoy – *A messenger sent by an organization to do business with another group of people.*

Media – *Newspapers, magazines, television, radio, the Internet, films, advertising.*

Sectarian – *Divisive, narrow and fixed opinions.*

Thought diary

Think of examples in the modern world where people fail to communicate. What are the consequences of not communicating? What possibilities can grow and develop when people do communicate?

The sound

What was the first human sound? Do some sounds have a more powerful effect on us than others? Do some sounds affect the brain while others affect the body or the heart?

In this unit we will explore the way sound communicates by looking at the Hindu tradition.

What do you think this painting by Edvard Munch is communicating?

Activity

1 You have one minute to think of your favourite-sounding word in the world. Go round the class and each say your word. Remember, it is not about the meaning of the word, but the sound of it.

2 Before they can read, children love to hear stories. They love the sound of the words, especially in **lullabies**, nursery rhymes and stories. Imagine you are babysitting for a 3 year-old. Create your own lullaby or short story. You can make up words if you want. Remember, the important thing is to create an interesting sound for the child and the meaning is not so important.

3 Some sounds can send a shiver down your spine, through fear, excitement or happiness; for example, a scream, a cheering crowd or beautiful singing. Can you think of other examples? Consider your favourite:

a sound in nature

b human sound

c animal sound

d night sound.

If you want to, you can try to communicate one of these sounds to the rest of the class, using sounds.

A Hindu View: Om

'Om' or 'Aum' (see the drawing below) is a sacred sound and a very important symbol in Hinduism. It is believed to be the original sound of the world, containing all other sounds. It represents **Brahman** – the Absolute – the source of all sound. It is made up of three Sanskrit letters, *au* and *m*. According to an ancient Hindu text:

> *The past, the present, and the future are all included in this one sound.*
>
> Mandukya Upanishad

Hindus use Om in daily life. A newborn child has the sacred **syllable** Om written on its tongue with honey. Om is chanted at the beginning of many prayers and mantras and some Hindus begin their day by uttering Om. The sacred symbol is often found at the head of letters and at the beginning of examination papers. Many Hindus wear the sign of Om as a **pendant** and the symbol is to be found in most Hindu temples.

Om is a mantra or prayer in itself. If repeated it can echo throughout the whole body to the centre of ourselves: the **atman** or the soul. While meditating, Hindus chant Om to create an inner vibration. This vibration can help a Hindu feel at one with themselves and the world.

Activity

Further activity

1 Using the information about Om, try to answer these questions:

  a Why is Om the most important sound and the most important symbol in Hinduism?

  b How do Hindus use the sound Om in their everyday lives?

2 Stand in a circle and say 'Oum' out loud as a group. Concentrate on sounding the 'A' from deep within your throat, 'U' from your mouth and 'M' on your lips. Repeat this three times. What effect did sounding Om have on you? Explore your reactions with the rest of the class.

Key Words

Atman – *The real self, the soul, present in all species of life.*

Brahman – *The ultimate reality, or God.*

Lullabies – *Soothing songs.*

Mantra – *A sacred sound repeated often.*

Pendant – *A hanging ornament usually worn around the neck.*

Syllable – *The vocal sounds that make up a word; for example, button has two syllables 'bu – tton'.*

Thought diary

Think of a sound that:

a) inspires your mind

b) touches your heart

c) affects your body.

Can you think of a sound that does all three?

The dance

What different ways are there of communicating? Are some forms of communication better than others? For example, is it better to communicate talking face to face or by sending a text message? If so, why? Is emailing a more effective way of communicating than talking on a telephone? Is a television report more effective than a newspaper article? Is a painting more effective than a photograph? Are movements, posture or dance more effective than words?

In this unit you will consider the power of different forms of communication by looking at the Islamic tradition.

Activity

1 Make up your own important message (for example, 'Recycle bottles' or 'Always wear a seatbelt'). It can be about anything. Decide how you would communicate it to:

a a 10-year-old and a 70-year-old, and

b a close friend and a complete stranger.

Would you always use the same method? Might there be other ways of communicating your message just as successfully as the one you used? Jot down your thoughts.

2 Think of times when you have felt very strong emotions about a person, an event or a situation. Write down some memories, thoughts or ideas about this feeling. It might have been a feeling of anger, love, hate, joy, fear, jealousy, excitement, embarrassment or guilt.

3 Now express this feeling using one of the following:

a a movement or a posture – sketch one or make one up that reflects how you felt;

b an image or a piece of artwork (you could make a collage);

c a song, a mime, or a poem;

d a sketch for a five-minute play/a text message/ or an email;

e ideas for a presentation in the form of a short talk.

Jot down at least one reason why you chose the method you did. Try to think of some reasons why you think it worked better than the others. If you want to, you can communicate it to the rest of the class using your chosen method.

The Whirling Dervishes – A Muslim view

Sacred music and dance have existed in Central Asia for centuries. Using dance as a form of prayer (or **dhikr** – 'remembering God' (**Allah**)), the **Sufis**, a branch of Islam, aim to communicate with Allah.

In the thirteenth century a great Sufi teacher called **Jalal al-Din al-Rumi** formed the **Mevlevi Dervish** community in Konya, Turkey. 'Mevlevi' means 'Wherever you turn you see the face of God'. His community or 'school' communicated its knowledge through the act of sacred dance.

Sufis experience the 'Turn', a controlled whirling dance, as a form of communication between heaven and Earth and between Allah and the **Dervish**.

A Dervish will turn twenty to thirty times a minute, with the right hand turned heavenward to receive Allah's **grace**, and the left turned down to communicate that grace to Earth.

Tradition holds that the Turn has been done at times when the planet has been in great need. Dervishes turn not for themselves, but for humanity and for the planet.

The Turn is always anti-clockwise; the right hand is palm-up, receiving, and the left hand is palm-down, grounding and communicating.

The full surface of the left foot never leaves the floor symbolizing that the Dervish has one foot in this world and one foot in the next.

To God belong the East and the West;
whithersoever ye turn, there is the face of God.
*For God is all-**pervading**, all-knowing.*

The Qur'an 2: 115

'Grace: Wherever you turn...'

Activity

1 In your own words, try to explain what the dance of the Whirling Dervishes is communicating.

2 Divide yourselves into four or five groups. Each group should be based on the method you found most effective in communicating your feelings in the previous activity. So:

- Group A will use a movement or a posture;
- Group B an image or a piece of artwork or a collage;
- Group C a song, a mime, or a poem;
- Group D a sketch for a five-minute play, a text message or an email;
- Group E a presentation in the form of short talk or lecture.

3 Working together as a group, communicate a Sufi idea – 'Wherever you turn you see the face of God' or 'The planet is in need' – to the rest of the class using your chosen method. Afterwards, discuss the advantages and disadvantages of working in a group. Which of the presentations do you think was best? Have a class vote.

Key Words

Allah – *God or the Divine in Islam.*

Dervish – *A member of a Sufi order who performs a whirling dance in worship of God.*

Dhikr – *Prayer of remembering Allah in the heart.*

Grace – *Means both 'fineness in movement' and 'a gift of loving help from God'.*

Jalal al-Din al-Rumi (1207–73) – *A great Sufi teacher, founder of the Mevlevi Dervishes.*

Mevlevi Dervishes – *A Sufi community who practise sacred dance.*

Pervading – *Spreading through every part.*

Sufis – *A branch of the Islamic faith.*

Thought diary

Research into the different ways other religions have communicated their ideas using dance and music (for example, Hindu dance; Christian hymn singing).

The image

What does a school uniform communicate about a school? What does it communicate about individual pupils at the school? In this unit, by looking at Sikhism, we will explore whether a person's image communicates anything about their personal beliefs and values.

Activity

1 You are going out with your friends. For some reason, on this particular occasion, you do not want to be the centre of attention and want to just blend into the background. Are there ways of presenting yourself so that you do not communicate *anything* about yourself?

Make a list, including clothing, haircut and posture, about how you would present yourself so as not to communicate *anything*. Sketch your ideas. Exchange your list and sketches with a friend. Is it possible *not* to communicate?

2 What are the two people in the photographs above trying to communicate about themselves by their appearance? Jot down some ideas. Compare them with a friend.

3 Are they wearing a 'uniform'? Is the goth in the photograph communicating the same message as other Goths? Are hiphop fans communicating anything about themselves by copying the image of *So Solid Crew?*

Make a list of the ways other groups of people communicate ideas about themselves through their appearances (for example, facial expressions).

4 It has been estimated that only 45 per cent of meaning comes from the words we use and the way we use them and 55 per cent of what we communicate is **non-verbal**. This means that we communicate information about ourselves in many different ways other than just by talking. Make a list of these different ways.

The five Ks – A Sikh view

During the sixteenth century the Sikh holy book the **Guru Granth Sahib Ji** established the **Khalsa**, a Punjabi word meaning the 'company of the faithful'. In order to show loyalty to the Sikh faith, a believer must become a member of the Khalsa. Sikhs are recognizable by their names and by their appearance. The Punjabi name for all members of the Khalsa is 'Singh' for a man meaning 'lion', and 'kaur' for a woman meaning 'princess'. The men have a common 'uniform' based on five elements known as 'the Five K's':

- **Kara**: a steel bracelet worn on the right wrist showing unity with God and the Khalsa.
- **Kirpan**: a sword symbolizing the courage to defend the faith and the poor.
- **Kesh**: long uncut hair – a symbol of strength and saintliness.
- **Kangha**: a wooden comb, representing cleanliness and inner purity.
- **Kachera**: under-trousers, representing agility and alertness.

The turban was added later and is the most important visible feature of a Sikh. Women also sometimes wear the wooden comb (kangha) and long hair (kesh) under a turban.

Activity

Further activity

1 Read the information on the five Ks. In your own words try to explain what beliefs and values the Sikh image is communicating. See if you can include some or all of the following Punjabi words: 'khalsa', 'kara', 'kirpan', 'kesh', 'kangha' and 'kachera' in your answer.

2 If you had to communicate your own beliefs through five items in your appearance, what would they be? Explain what each one would be saying about you. Draw your symbols.

3 Choose one other religion and research how followers communicate their faith through their appearance.

Key Words

Guru Granth Sahib Ji – *Sikh sacred scriptures.*

Khalsa – *A Punjabi word for the 'company of the faithful'.*

Non-verbal – *Communication without words.*

Thought diary

Can you express yourself individually? Or do we only express the beliefs and values of various groups?

The word

How many words have you spoken so far today? Do you use more words some days than others? Do you sometimes 'waste' words? Are some words more important than others? Do you sometimes use 'bad language' – gossip, swear, lie, abuse, criticize, **slander** or insult others? The words we choose to use and the way we use them are powerful tools of communication.

In this unit we will explore the power of the spoken word by looking at the Buddhist view.

Bad language?

Look at these expressions. You may think that they are very ordinary 'soft' swear words but look at what is behind what you are communicating:

- *'Blimey!'* comes from 'Blind me!'
- *'Stone me!'* refers to the act of stoning someone to death.
- *'Damn you!'* is calling God to send someone to eternal damnation in Hell.
- *'Crikey!'* comes from 'Christ's key'.
- *'Strewth'* comes from 'God's truth'.

When you use some swear words, what you are doing is calling a Higher Power to bear upon the 'object of your scorn'.

Today for many people these sorts of expressions do not communicate what they once did, for example, 'Go to hell!' or 'God Almighty!' Many religious followers, however, think it is wrong to speak without respect, or to use bad language about things considered holy. This is known as **blasphemy**.

Activity

1 Strong swear words often refer to parts of the body or bodily functions – particularly bleeding, excreting or sexual activity. What do you think this communicates about our view of the human body? With a friend discuss whether the human body deserves such language used about it?

2 Write down as many examples as you can of the way words are used to communicate something (for example, text messages, adverts or film credits).

3 Apply these words: 'love,' 'hate', 'damn', 'heavenly' to all of the eight words below:

Chocolates
Pets
Shopping
Homework
My mother
My best friend
Living
The world

Does the meaning of a word change when you use it with a different word? (for example, does the word 'love' change in different combinations: 'love my mother; 'love chocolate'?). Jot down your most powerful expression using these combinations.

4 Do words have no meaning on their own? Or is their meaning created according to the word(s) they are used *with*?

5 Make up your own list of eight words. Apply 'love', 'hate', 'damn' and 'heavenly' to your list.

6 Think about the way you use language in order to be liked, admired, to get what you want or to get your own way. Write down any observations you might have.

Right Speech – A Buddhist view

A Buddhist saying is: 'If you cannot control your mouth, there is no way you can hope to control your mind.'

A key teaching in Buddhism is **Right Speech**: avoiding language that is abusive and hurtful. It means not telling lies, telling tales, or backbiting. Right Speech is one part of the Buddhist beliefs in not causing harm to any other living thing. Buddhists recognize that words used in the wrong context can have a harmful effect and words used in the right context can communicate positive qualities like trust and compassion. Buddhism teaches that we should let words reflect our desire to help, not harm others. Before we speak, we should focus on *why* we want to speak.

If you cannot control your mouth there is no way you can hope to control your mind

Activity

Further activity

1 Do you always use words helpfully?

Look at the following instructions taken from **The Patimokkha**, an ethical code for Buddhist Monks. This will be your guidebook. With a friend, discuss the following questions:

- Do I speak at the right time or not?
- Do I speak of facts or not?
- Do I speak gently or harshly?
- Do I speak positive words or not?
- Do I speak with a kindly heart, or am I inwardly **malicious**?

2 Try to think of situations where a Buddhist might find it difficult to follow these guidelines: for example, telling a lie to get your best friend out of trouble.

3 Think of a) a time when you could answer 'yes' to the five questions and b) a time when you could answer 'no'. Share your thoughts with the class.

4 Why do Buddhists believe that, 'If you cannot control your mouth, there is no way you can hope to control your mind'?

Key Words

Blasphemy – *To speak without respect/use bad language against things considered holy.*

Malicious – *Meaning to hurt someone.*

Right speech – *The Buddhist belief that we should not use abusive or hurtful language.*

Slander – *To speak badly about someone using lies.*

The Patimokkha – *A code of behaviour for Buddhist Monks.*

Thought diary

Over the next week watch your language!

The message

At the beginning of this chapter we saw that when communication breaks down, violence and even war may follow. Why does this happen in 'the media age', 'the information age'? Are people getting the wrong information and the wrong messages? In this unit we will explore messages and their meaning and how one religion looks to a world where people live in peace.

Activity

The total television audience for the 64 matches at the 2002 World Cup in Japan and South Korea was an estimated 50 billion viewers: an average of 780 million viewers per game. Two billion people watched the final live between Germany and Brazil. This is roughly one-third of the world's population! The **globalization** of communications technology has caused the nature of communication to change.

For the first time in human history a concentration of human attention on one specific event can occur among billions of people.

1 Read the following carefully and jot down any thoughts that come to mind when considering whether the media communicates positive or negative messages.

- An estimated £10 billion is spent worldwide on pornography every year.
- The television programme *Pop Idol* had 10 million viewers, while *Unreported World*, a programme about injustice around the world, had less than one million viewers.
- UK television is 60 per cent British, 35 per cent American, 3 per cent Australian and 2 per cent the rest of the world (for example, Africa, India, Asia).
- 35,000 people starve to death every day whilst Europeans spend £8 billion a year on ice-cream.

2 Make a list of the positive effects of modern communication systems (for example, television helps people understand the world better; the Internet connects people around the world).

3 Does someone with access to a television, a mobile phone and the Internet treat other people and the world around them better than somebody without access to these technologies? Give reasons for your answer.

The Messiah – A Jewish view

In Jewish belief, human history will be brought to an end when God communicates his existence to everyone on Earth and takes up his dwelling place in the world. This new age is to be brought about by a **Messiah**.

Jews believe the Messiah will be a man, a descendant of **King David**, not a god. He will have great qualities of wisdom, **piety** and leadership.

The time of the Messiah is sometimes called the 'world to come'. It is expected to be a time of peace and unity throughout the world.

The **Prophets** Micah and Isaiah, two of the greatest communicators in the **Tenakh**, the Jewish Bible, describe some of the things that will happen when the Messiah comes:

> *They shall beat their swords into ploughshares and their spears into pruning hooks. Nation shall not lift up sword against nation, nor shall they train any more for war.*
>
> Micah 4: 3

> *The wolf shall live with the lamb, and the leopard shall lie down with the kid; and the calf and the young lion and the fatling together; and a little child shall lead them.*
>
> Isaiah 11

'Once a photograph of the earth taken from space is available a new idea as powerful as any in history will be let loose' (Sir Fred Hoyle, astronomer). What might this 'new idea' be do you think?

Activity

Further activity

1 **Reformist Jews** believe that 'the coming of the Messiah' is a symbolic term for a time when everyone in the world will live in peace. Imagine you were the head of an international media company. You have been given an hour's time to show a programme to the whole world based on Isaiah and Micah's visions of peace. It will appear on every television and computer screen in the world.

- In small groups, do a plan for your programme.
- Use pie charts/flow diagrams/picture boards to help you get organized.
- Concentrate on your methods and your message.
- Remember that you must appeal to all people, irrespective of their age, religion or culture.

2 Research activity: Find out what other religions teach about peace and/or the coming of a Messiah.

Key Words

Globalization – *The linking up of the world by communication and trade.*

King David – *Hebrew king.*

Messiah – *A person who brings new ways and saves people from difficulty.*

Piety – *Respect and devotion especially towards religious duty and God.*

Prophets – *Jewish holy men.*

Reformist Jews – *Jews who believe the coming of the Messiah is a symbolic term for the ideal of the world living in unity.*

Tenakh – *The Jewish Bible.*

Thought diary

Perhaps you might try to watch a programme or film from a part of the world you would not normally come across. Reflect on whether you considered anything differently after watching it.

Assessment

In this chapter we have begun to think about the importance of communication and the many different ways in which we can communicate.

Communication?: Write your own caption for this photograph

Have you observed anything about how you have communicated with others as you have explored the activities in this chapter?

Here are a few questions that you might have thought about in each unit:

1. *The breakdown – Why is communicating difficult?*
2. *A Hindu view – Can a sound be everlasting?*
3. *A Muslim view – How do we communicate through movement?*
4. *A Sikh view – Are images always beliefs?*
5. *A Buddhist view – What is bad language?*
6. *A Jewish view – Does communication make for a better or a worse world?*

Reflecting on your progress

1. *To help you reflect on what you have learned from this chapter, look back on your work, or in your Thought diary, and write a few lines on each of the following areas, giving reasons to improve your answers:*
   - (a) What I enjoyed. Why?
   - (b) What I found difficult. Why?

2. *Pick an idea that you liked and try to explain it clearly to another person. Think about:*
   - Where the idea came from.
   - What the idea is about.
   - Why you like the idea.
   - The *best* way to explain it to someone else.

3. *In your Thought diary, copy down five* ***skills*** *that you have used most during this chapter from the following list:*
   - I listened to others well.
   - I gave reasons for my views.
   - I expressed my ideas clearly.
   - I tried to imagine other people's point of view.
   - I developed my writing or artistic skills.
   - I investigated a new topic well.
   - I made new ideas for myself.
   - I kept on task well.
   - I used lots of imagination.
   - I cared about the feelings of other people.

4. *What facts did you learn? What do you understand now that you did not know about before? Make a spider diagram or poster to show your thoughts.*

Test yourself

1. *'A uniform does not communicate anything about what the individual thinks.' How might a Sikh respond to this comment? Do you agree with their view? Does our image communicate anything about us? What does a Sikh's appearance communicate about their beliefs and values? [Level 5 – AT2]*

2. *Why is sound an important part of communication? Explain the importance of the sound 'Om' in Hindu belief. Try to use some Hindu terms such as 'mantra' and 'atman' in your answer. [Level 6 – AT2]*

3. *What is communicated about Sufi beliefs by the Whirling Dervish dance? [Level 7 – AT2]*

4. *Have modern communication technologies created a global village? Try to give different points of view in your answer and explain your own opinion. Could they be used to communicate peace and unity? (Hint: See pages 84 and 85) [Level 8 – AT2]*

Where next?

1. *Look at the list of skills above. Choose three that you want to improve on in the future. Perhaps you could note them down in your Thought diary. (How could you improve them? Is there someone who could give you suggestions? Is there some way of reminding yourself?)*

2. *Think about the topic you enjoyed most. What could you do to investigate it further? Are there any websites or books that could help you find out more?*

Well done!

You know more, have thought more and have improved your skills.

KEEP GOING!

Christianity key facts

Christianity – what is it?

Where and when did it begin?

Palestine, a part of the Roman Empire, now Israel. Jesus born between 6 and 4 BCE; religion began after his death approximately 29 CE.

Who founded it?

Jesus Christ (title from the Greek meaning 'Messiah', a Hebrew title meaning 'chosen by God').

Followers

Known as disciples (meaning 'followers') particularly twelve Apostles (meaning 'messengers') who were Jesus's closest companions: Simon (who later became known as Peter), his brother Andrew, James, John, Philip, Bartholomew, Thomas, Matthew, James son of Alphaeus, Thaddaeus, Simon the Zealot and Judas Iscariot.

Special writings

The Bible is made up of 66 books, 39 of which were written before Jesus and 27 of which were by followers after his death. These sections are known as 'Testaments' meaning 'agreement'. The Roman Catholics include a further section called The Apocrypha, literature covering the period of history between the writing of the Old and New Testaments. Some Christians believe that the Bible contains the unaltered word of God and literally believe every word. Other Christians believe that, although the Bible is inspired by God, it was written by people and is therefore open to error.

Symbol

The Christian cross.

Places of worship

Christians usually meet for regular worship on Sundays, the day on which they remember the resurrection of Jesus. The central part of this worship for most Christians is the Eucharist, meaning 'thanksgiving'; an event remembering the last meal that Jesus shared with his disciples on earth in which he broke bread and shared wine saying that these elements were his body and blood. Christians share this meal together in memory of Jesus's sacrifice on the cross. Worship can take different forms but usually involves readings from the Bible, prayers, hymns of praise and a sermon from the person leading the service, who may be a priest or vicar.

Pilgrimages

There are many sites of pilgrimages for Christians throughout the world. In Israel, these are centred around events in the life of Jesus, such as the Church of the Nativity on Bethlehem and the Church of the Holy Sepulchre, built over the tomb where his body lay.

In other parts of the world Christians visit scenes of visions and miracles. Lourdes in France is an example of this and is now regarded by many as a place of healing. Roman Catholics make a special point of visiting Rome, not only for its historical significance in the development of Christianity, but also because it is the home of the Pope.

Festivals

The Church year begins on 30 November, St Andrew's Day, and is followed by celebrations of the main events in Jesus's life.

- Advent – 24 days leading up to birth of Jesus; Christians use this as a time of preparation and remember the visit of the angel to Mary.
- Christmas – a joyful festival when Christians give thanks for Jesus's birth.
- Epiphany – the visit of the wise men to Jesus at his birth; it is celebrated as Christmas by Orthodox Christians; it also remembers Jesus's baptism.
- Lent – the time following his baptism when Jesus prepared for his ministry; Christians use this as a special time of penitence to get ready for the holiest part of the year.
- Easter – Jesus's death and resurrection, events central to Christianity.
- Ascension – the time when Jesus returned to Heaven.
- Whitsun – a traditional time of baptism when Christians remember the giving of the Holy Spirit and the beginning of the Church.
- Trinity – the rest of the year when Christians recall Jesus's ministry and teaching.
- Saints days are also celebrated by different denominations during the year.

What's it all about?

After Jesus's death, the disciples formed communities that became known as 'churches'; this did not refer to buildings but to the people themselves.

Followers became known as Christians and they met together in their houses to remember Jesus and his message.

These churches kept in touch by letters, 21 of which remain in the New Testament.

By 65 CE the persecution of Christians had begun but rather than wipe the religion out it helped the faith to spread throughout the Roman Empire and beyond.

In 412 CE, under the Emperor Constantine, Christianity became accepted and later became the religion of the Roman Empire. Missionaries were sent to other countries carrying the message.

From 1054 CE, the Church began to divide into different groups; today the main divisions are Orthodox, Roman Catholic and Protestant. The Protestant Church is made up of a variety of denominations. These all follow the same basic beliefs as those above but choose to worship in different ways. Today the Ecumenical Movement seeks to unite the churches rather than stress the differences.

What do Christians believe?

Roman Catholics accept and follow the teachings of the Pope, believed to be the direct successor to the Apostle, Peter, who is regarded as the first Bishop of Rome. The Orthodox and Protestant Churches take their authority from the Bible as the word of God.

The main beliefs of Christians are set out in the Apostles' Creed (from the Latin 'credo' meaning 'I believe'). This is a prayer based on the early teachings of the Apostles.

These include:

- Belief in the Trinity, an idea to explain how three persons make up one God – God the Father, God the Son and God the Holy Spirit.
- Belief that God the Father is the creator and father of all things.
- Belief that God the Son is Jesus Christ, born to a virgin called Mary; he lived on earth and was crucified, died and was buried and rose again three days later. He now reigns in Heaven with God the Father and will return to judge the living and the dead.
- Belief that God as the Holy Spirit is God's power and inspiration in a person's life and this was given to Jesus's disciples after he had returned to Heaven.
- Belief in the catholic church. In this sense, the word 'catholic' means 'universal' or 'worldwide' and the word 'church' refers to all the Christians who form part of this fellowship throughout the world.
- Belief in the 'communion of saints', referring to the relationship between all Christians, alive as well as dead.
- Christians believe that anyone who is truly sorry for what they have done wrong can be forgiven by God providing they are sincerely determined not to repeat the sin.
- Belief that there is life after death for all believers.

Famous twentieth-century Christians

Martin Luther King (1929–68) worked for Civil Rights in America through non-violent protests.

Desmond Tutu (1939–present) first black archbishop in South Africa who chaired the Truth and Reconciliation Committee following the end of Apartheid.

Mother Teresa (1910–1997) worked with the poor and dying on the streets of Calcutta, India.

Christianity today has spread throughout the world and is the principle religion of many countries.

Islam key facts

Islam – what is it?

Where and when did it begin?
In Arabia during the early seventh century CE.

Who founded it?
The Prophet Muhammad (pbuh) who lived 570–633 CE.

Special writings
The Qur'an is the basic source of all Islamic teachings and laws.

The Hadith – the teachings, sayings and actions of the Prophet Muhammad (pbuh) recorded and collected by his devoted companions – explain the Qur'anic verses.

Symbol
A crescent moon.

Places of worship
Muslims can practise their religion anywhere, but especially at home or in a mosque.

Pilgrimages
The Hajj to Makkah (also spelt Mecca) leads to the Ka'bah built by the Prophet Abraham over 3,000 years ago. Jerusalem is also considered a Muslim holy city.

Festivals
The most important event in the Muslim calendar is Ramadan (the ninth month of the Islamic year) – a holy month of fasting. The beginning of the next month (Id-ul-Fitr) is a time of celebration when people give money to the poor (zakah).

What's it all about?

Muhammad (pbuh)
The Prophet Muhammad (pbuh) was born in Makkah, Arabia. He came from a noble family, led a perfect life and set an example to those around him. At the age of 40, while meditating in the Cave of Hira, he received his first revelation from God through the angel Jibra'il. For the next 23 years Muhammad's (pbuh) revelations continued and he preached his message across Arabia. His revelations were written down by scribes and formed the Islamic holy book, the Qur'an. Although he and his followers were persecuted and had to face severe hardships, they finally converted the pagan city of Makkah into the centre of the Muslim faith. Within a century of Muhammad's (pbuh) death Islam had spread from Spain in the west to China in the east.

What do Muslims believe?
'Submission to the will of God'. This word comes from the same root as the Arabic word 'salam' which means 'peace'. The religion of Islam is the surrender to the 'will of Allah' – the complete acceptance of the teachings and guidance of God. The faith believes in the one God who created the universe. Throughout the world Muslims prefer to use the Arabic word 'Allah' for 'God'. They believe that every action done with the awareness that it fulfils the 'will of Allah' is an act of worship. Nevertheless the following specific acts of worship, called the 'Pillars of Islam', make up the basic framework of daily life:

Where is Islam practised?
Islam began in its present form 1400 years ago in Arabia but quickly spread to become a global religion. Today there are over 1.2 billion Muslims worldwide with around 2 million Muslims in Britain. The countries with the largest Islamic populations are in Asia, particularly Indonesia, Pakistan, Bangladesh and India. Islam is a religion for all people whatever race or background they might be. Muslims are to be found on every continent in the world and Islam is the main religion in Afghanistan, Malaysia, Azerbaijan, Turkmenistan, Uzbekistan, Iran, Iraq, Syria, Jordan, the Arab States, and Turkey and in Africa in Egypt, Algeria, Tunisia, Djibouti, Gambia, Guinea, Libya, Mali, Mauritanian, Morocco, Niger, Somalia, Senegal, Sudan and Zanzibar. Large Muslim communities are also to be found in Europe, particularly Albania, Bosnia and Macedonia, elsewhere in Europe immigrant communities of Muslims exist. In the Americas the Islamic population has greatly increased in recent years both from conversions and the immigration of Muslims from other parts of the world.

Pillars of Islam

1 The declaration of faith
'I bear witness that there is none worthy of worship except Allah and that Muhammad (pbuh) is His servant and messenger'; the prophethood of Muhammad (pbuh) obliges individual Muslims to follow his example in every way.

2 Prayer
Muslims must pray five times daily: at dawn, at noon, in the mid-afternoon, at dusk, and after dark. The world, according to Islam, is a place of trial and we are being judged in it. Prayer purifies the heart, strengthens faith and helps control any temptation to do wrong.

3 Zakah
Muslims must pay a percentage of their earnings to help the poor and needy. This is called zakah. It shows that everything we possess belongs to Allah and therefore anyone in need has a share in it.

4 Fasting
Once each year, during the month of Ramadan, Muslims observe the fast. From dawn to sunset Muslims must not eat, drink, smoke or have intimate marital relationships. Fasting is much more than not eating or drinking but a period of total physical and emotional cleansing when a Muslim struggles against all evil thoughts and desires (jihad).

5 Hajj
Muslims try to go on Hajj at least once in a lifetime provided they have the means to do so. Hajj requires that people temporarily put their normal daily lives on hold and together with millions of other pilgrims of all races and nations a Muslim has an opportunity to stand in front of Allah alone.

How is Islam different?
Islam is not a new religion. It contains, in essence, the same message and guidance revealed to the prophets Abraham, Moses and Jesus. Muslims believe that the message revealed to Muhammad (pbuh), the last Prophet, is Islam in its complete and final form. In Islam there is no hierarchy of priests or complicated rituals. Everybody may read and learn from the Qur'an directly and put its teachings into use in everyday life.

Judaism key facts

Judaism – what is it?

Where and when did it begin?

Judaism is the religion of the Jews and it began over 3000 years ago at the time of Abraham when God made an agreement with him. This agreement or covenant, was that God would look after his people, keep them safe.

Special writings

The Hebrew Bible is made up of many books. The Torah, the first five books of the Bible, contains the teachings. These are considered to be very important because it tells Jewish people how they should live their lives, it gives them rules they should follow. The Neviim tells of the Prophets and their lives, how God spoke through them. The Ketuvim are writings that glorify God and are often used in worship.

Torah
Genesis
Exodus
Leviticus
Numbers
Deuteronomy

Neviim
Joshua
Judges
1 and 2 Samuel
1 and 2 Kings
Isaiah
Jeremiah
Ezekiel
Hosea
Joel
Amos
Obadiah
Jonah
Micah
Nahum
Habbakuk
Zephaniah
Haggai
Zechariah
Malachai

Ketuvim
Psalms
Proverbs
Job
Song of Songs
Ruth
Lamentations
Ecclesiastes
Esther
Ruth
Daniel
Ezra
Nehamiah
1 and 2
Chronicles

You may recognize some of these books as forming part of the Old Testament in the Bible. For Jews these are not a part of the Old Testament; they are part of their holy Bible and show God's promise to them.

Another important holy book is the Talmud. This contains the ideas and teachings of great Jewish scholars and is often referred to when people are unsure about how they should behave in a situation.

Where do Jews worship?

Jews worship in a synagogue, the word literally means meeting place, and it is a focal point of the Jewish community. Synagogues are always built facing toward Jerusalem because this is where Solomon built his Temple before it was destroyed and the Jews were forced to leave their homeland and live in Babylon.

The synagogue is not just used as a place of worship, children go there to learn Hebrew and about the Torah. It can be somewhere to meet and talk through problems.

Inside a synagogue you will notice several distinctive features. There may be an area for men to pray and a separate area for women. Some Jews believe that women can distract men from prayer.

You will also notice a cupboard known as the Ark. This is important because in here the Torah scrolls are kept. When the Torah scrolls are not being used they are kept in special covers.

There will also be the bimah. This is a raised platform where the Torah sits during a service; it is higher than everyone else to show that God's word is more important.

Above the Ark you will see a light burning. This light never goes out and represents God looking after his people. He is always with them. Another feature you will notice are two stone tablets. These will have Hebrew writing on them and they represent the ten sayings that God gave to Moses on the top of Mount Sinai.

Also in the synagogue you will see an important Jewish symbol, the Star of David. This represents a shield against evil.

Festivals

Shabbat

This is a weekly celebration remembering God creating the world in six days and resting on the seventh. It begins at sunset on Friday and ends twenty five hours later. Traditionally Jews stop working for the whole day; it is a day of rest.

Rosh Hashanah and Yom Kippur

This marks the New Year for Jews and is a time when they think about the things they have done wrong; they say sorry and ask for forgiveness from God at Yom Kippur, the Day of Atonement. On this day Jews will fast and pray.

Sukkot

This is a festival about thanking God for all the things He has given his people.

Simchat Torah

This is an important celebration for Jews as it marks the beginning of the reading of the Torah in the synagogue. The Jews thank God for the law that He has given them.

Hannukah

Hannukah lasts for eight days at the start of December and is known as the Festival of Lights remembering a miracle when Judas defeated the Greek army and reclaimed the Temple for the Jews. Judas and his people threw out all the Greek idols and looked to relight the Menorah, the seven-headed candle. This light in the Temple was never allowed to go out but there was only enough oil for it to keep burning for one day. However, the light stayed alight whilst the Jews waited for more oil to arrive in Jerusalem.

Purim

This celebration remembers how good will overcome evil and the bravery of Esther, who, through careful planning and with God's help, saved the Jewish people from death.

Pesach

This festival, often referred to as Passover, remembers how God saved his people from the Egyptians, and how his people wandered for 40 years in the desert before claiming the promised land. This festival remembers God's power as He caused the ten plagues which led to the Exodus of the Israelites from Egypt.

Shavuot

This celebration remembers how Moses was given the Law by God.

What do Jews believe?

Jewish belief is captured in the Shema, a statement of faith that is said each morning and each evening. This can be found in Deuteronomy 6:4–5.

'Hear O Israel! The Lord is our God, the Lord is one! And you shall love the Lord your God with all your heart and with all your soul and with all your might.'

This is written on a piece of parchment and can be found in a mezuzah, nailed to the doorpost of a Jewish home and outside each room except the bathroom. Whenever a Jew enters a room they will touch the mezuzah to remind themselves of the Shema.

For Jews, God is everywhere. He created the world and can act within the world to help His people.

They follow the Ten Commandments found in Exodus 20:1–17, and other laws known as the mitzvot.

Jewish people follow strict laws about food. They have foods that are kosher, or permitted, and non-kosher foods – food which should not be eaten.

Foods that are kosher are:

- Fish that have fins and scales such as cod.
- Animals that have cloven hooves and eat grass.
- Birds such as chicken; birds of prey are not allowed.

Buddhism key facts

Buddhism – what is it?

Where and when did it begin?

Buddhism began in India about 2500 years ago.

Who founded it?

The Buddha, who lived 563–483 BCE.

Special writings

There are several types of Buddhism, each of which have different texts. Two very important ones are: 'The Pali Canon' and 'The Perfection of Wisdom'. Both are very long and describe the Buddha's life story, how to be a Buddhist, and what the truth about life really is.

Symbol

An eight-spoked wheel.

Places of worship

Buddhists can practise their religion anywhere, but especially at home or in temples. Monks live in 'viharas' or monasteries.

Pilgrimages

Buddhists might go on pilgrimages to many special places, but four are particularly important: where the Buddha was born, became enlightened, taught his first sermon, and died.

Festivals

Buddhist festivals can differ from country to country. However, one major festival that all Buddhists celebrate is on the full moon in May. It marks three occasions in the Buddha's life – his birth, enlightenment and death.

What's it all about?

The Buddha

Siddhartha Gautama was born into a very wealthy family, but as he grew older he realized that his great fortune would never stop him suffering from old age, sickness and death. At 29 he decided to leave all of his luxury and his family behind, and set out to see if there was a solution to these sufferings that all human beings face. For six years he learned all he could from many great teachers, but even they could not give him a solution. Eventually he sat down under a tree in Bodh Gaya (in North India), and meditated all night. By morning he had understood the deepest truths about life, and he was free from ever having to suffer again; he had become 'enlightened'. From this point on he became known as 'the Buddha' which means 'one who is fully awake' to the truth. For the next 45 years he taught other people how to become enlightened and free themselves from suffering. He died at the age of 80 leaving others to carry on his teachings.

What do Buddhists believe?

Buddhists believe that the Buddha had found a solution to life's sufferings, and that if they follow his teachings they can help themselves – and others – to find perfect peace and happiness. Buddhists call Buddhism 'the dharma' which means 'the truth' or 'law' about the way things really are. The Buddha summarized his teachings in 'The Four Noble Truths':

1. Life always involves suffering of some sort. Even when we feel happy, it never seems to last.
2. The cause of this suffering is our own ignorance or 'wrong-thinking' about ourselves. We should recognize that our own minds are full of wrong ideas, and, because of them we end up being driven by desires that stop us from realizing the truth.
3. However, the cause of this suffering – our ignorance and desires – can be 'blown out' ('nirvana') by realizing the truth. We can then be free from all suffering, and be perfectly happy and peaceful.
4. We can achieve nirvana by perfecting eight special skills or 'following the Eight Fold Path'. (That is why there are eight spokes in the Buddhist symbol – eight skills that frcc you from the 'wheel of life').

The eight special skills involve:

- Morality – learning how to act in a good way (good karma) and avoid bad actions (bad karma). This includes being kind, non-violent and honest to everyone, for example
- Wisdom – working hard to understand Buddhist teachings about the truth of life. This includes studying the words of the Buddha and seeing how they make sense in our own lives
- Meditation – training the mind to be calm and focused, so that we can realize the truth of the Buddhist teachings through direct experience and not just as 'an idea'.

How is Buddhism different?

Buddhism differs from other religions in several ways. It teaches that there is no God, no 'unchanging soul', and that the way to find deep and true happiness is *our own responsibility*. The Buddha is seen as a very special man, but he is not regarded as 'being alive today' by most Buddhists. His image in temples is often used as an inspiration or a focus for meditation. However, it is important to realize that there are many kinds of Buddhists, and that they might have different views about what their religion teaches and how it might be practised.

Where is Buddhism practised?

Buddhism began in India, but spread to many other countries over the centuries, particularly in Asia. Tibet, Mongolia, Thailand, Laos, Vietnam, Sri Lanka are all Buddhist countries today and both Japan and China were heavily influenced by Buddhism in their past. The dharma has also became very popular in the West in the last 50 years; there are Buddhist centres in most European countries and many in America.

Whenever Buddhism moved to another country it met many new influences. These countries would already have their own religions, languages, festivals and traditions. Conscqucntly Buddhism would adapt to fit in with its new surroundings and this explains why there are many different types of Buddhism today. All forms of Buddhism, however, still follow the basic teachings of the Four Noble Truths and the life of the Buddha.

Famous Buddhists: The Dalai Lama

Perhaps the most famous Buddhist in the world is Tenzin Gyatso, the fourteenth Dalai Lama (meaning Ocean of Wisdom). He is a Tibetan Buddhist monk who is regarded as the fourteenth reincarnation of the first Dalai Lama (a great spiritual teacher) who lived 600 years ago. Buddhists all over the world see the fourteenth Dalai Lama as a great example of someone who is kind, compassionate and wise.

The Dalai Lama used to live in Tibet, ruling his huge country (the size of Western Europe) even when he was a teenager. However, when the Chinese invaded Tibet in 1950, the fourteenth Dalai Lama was forced to flee to safety nine years later and he now heads the 'Tibetan Government in Exile' in northern India. Despite all the terrible things that his people have suffered under Chinese rule in Tibet, the Dalai Lama still strongly believes in finding non – violent solutions to the problem. Compassion and ahimsa, or non-violence, are very important parts of Buddhist belief and practise.

Hinduism key facts

Hinduism – what is it?

It is important to realize that there are many ways of believing and worshipping in Hinduism. The religion is grouped around the central beliefs which many Hindus share. For this reason many Hindus prefer their religion to be known 'Sanatan Dharma' (eternal laws or teaching) as they believe this reflects the fact that it is more a way of life than a religion which often reflects the way they eat, whom they marry and even the jobs they do. The Hindu tradition is very diverse. Many Hindus will worship in different ways or consider certain festivals as special.

Where and when did it begin?

Hinduism is one of the world's oldest religions. People were worshipping in the Indus Valley in India over 3000 years ago.

Who founded it?

There was no one founder. There is evidence of its existence over 4500 years ago among the people of the Indus Valley.

Special writings

There are several special writings. Different Hindus consider some writings more important than others. The oldest writings are the Vedas, which contain hymns, stories of gods and goddesses, poetry and religious and social laws. The Upanishads are hymns and poems that discuss questions about life. The Ramayana and the Mahabharata are two special poems. The Bhagavad Gita is an important part of the Mahabharata.

Symbol

The Aum. This is considered to be the first sound at the start of creation.

Places of worship

Although Hindus will often go to the mandirs, or temples, for festivals, most will also worship daily at their own home shrine. Some of the mandirs are very large and elaborate, like Swaminarayan Mandir in Neasden, others are small and simple. Each temple is really a house for its particular god. It is the priest's duty to look after the image of the god (murti) and to treat it like a very special visitor. Worship in the home is important for many Hindus. There will often be a shrine to the family's chosen diety. It may be on a shelf or in the corner of a room. Here the family will perform daily worship or puja.

Pilgrimages

Most of the places of pilgrimage are in India. Varanasi on the River Ganga (also called the Ganges) and the town of Vrindavan where Krishna lived as a child are especially important. The river Ganga is an especially important place for pilgrimage. Many pilgrims go there to spinkle ashes or to say prayers for the dead.

Festivals

There are many Hindu festivals as all the gods have days when they are remembered and worshipped. Not all Hindus celebrate every festival. There are two main reasons for Hindu festivals:

- To celebrate the lives of gods and goddesses.
- To celebrate the seasons.

In Britain most Hindus celebrate Divali, which remembers the story of Rama and Sita. It is often called the festival of lights and can last as long as five days.

The festival of Holi is in the spring and is usually a time for fun. Hindus tell stories of the practical jokes that Krishna played and often throw coloured water at each other.

Raksha Bandhan is often celebrated in August. It is a time when brothers and sisters show their love and affection for each other. They will often exchange gifts including a rakhi (friendship bracelet).

What's it all about?

Hindus believe in one 'Supreme being', or soul, from whom everything comes. This great soul is called Brahman. Brahman is like the root of a tree and everything else in the world is the branches and leaves. There are many different gods or goddesses (deities), which represent different aspects of Brahman's nature and power.

In the temple and home shrine Hindus will often focus their worship on statues of the gods and goddesses. These are called murtis.

What do Hindus believe?

Hindus consider their religion as a way of life. There are duties and codes (dharma), which everyone is expected to follow no matter how young or old. Every person has their own individual soul, or atman. It is this atman that moves through a cycle of birth, death and rebirth and so forms the process of reincarnation.

Since each living being has an atman, many Hindus are vegetarians and consider it wrong to kill an animal, as they are part of the same spirit. The cow is an animal which is considered very special and many Hindus will not eat beef or wear leather.

Hindus believe that how a person is reincarnated depends upon their 'karma'. This is the law of cause and effect. Hindus believe that whatever they do their actions will have a result in the future. The aim of a Hindu's life is to break free of this endless chain of birth, death and rebirth to achieve 'moksha' where the atman becomes one with Brahman.

The Bhagavad Gita tells of three pathways to follow which will lead to this aim:

1. Knowledge – to study the special books of Hinduism and to think deeply about their teachings.
2. Yoga – to carry out exercises for the mind and the body.
3. Bhakti – to show a love for God through prayer and service.

Famous twentieth century Hindus

Mahatma Gandhi (1869–1948) was a political and religious leader in India. In his campaign for fair treatment and equality he always used non-violent actions. His peaceful approach and words have been a major influence on many twentieth-century Hindus and non-Hindus.

Sikhism key facts

Sikhism – what is it?

Where and when did it begin?

Sikhism began in India in the fifteenth century CE.

Who founded it?

Guru Nanak Dev Ji, who lived 1469–1539 CE (guru means teacher).

Special writings

The main book for Sikhs is called the Guru Granth Sahib Ji. It contains the teachings of Guru Nanak Dev Ji and the nine gurus who followed after him.

Symbol

The Khanda.

Places of worship

Sikhs worship in the home and in a building called a gurdwara. The word gurdwara means 'doorway to the guru'. Every gurdwara has a langar. This is a kitchen that serves free food.

Pilgrimages

A special place for Sikhs is Amritsar, in the Punjab in India. Guru Arjan Dev Ji built what is known as the Golden Temple. It is where the Guru Granth Sahib Ji is kept.

Festivals

Sikhs have many festivals. They include Divali, celebrating the festival of light; Baisakhi, which celebrates the forming of the Khalsa (Sikh community); and gurpurbs, which are festivals that remember the gurus.

What's it all about?

Guru Nanak Dev Ji was brought up as a Hindu. However as he grew up he was influenced by both Hinduism and Islam and became discontented with the beliefs and practices of these two religions. It is believed that one day Guru Nanak Dev Ji went to bathe in a river and disappeared. He was said to have drowned, but after three days he miraculously returned. Guru Nanak Dev Ji claimed that he met with God who revealed to him that there was no difference between Hindus and Muslims; all people belong to God.

Guru Nanak Dev Ji travelled around spreading his teachings. Nine gurus followed after him and continued to spread his message:

1 Guru Angad Dev Ji (1504–52) – he translated the hymns of Guru Nanak into a language called Gurmukhi.

2 Guru Amar Das Ji (1479–1574) – he spread many teachings of Sikhism. He developed the idea of the langar.

3 Guru Ram Das Ji (1534–81) – he founded the city of Amritsar.

4 Guru Arjan Dev Ji (1563–1606) – he was the first Sikh martyr (someone who dies for their beliefs). He collected together the teachings of the gurus and built the Golden Temple at Amritsar.

5 Guru Har Gobind Ji (1595–1644) – he trained Sikhs to fight so they could defend their faith.

6 Guru Hari Rai Ji (1630–61) – he worked towards spreading peace. He is remembered for his caring and generous nature.

7 Guru Hari Krishan Ji (1656–64) – he died as a child.

8 Guru Tegh Behadur Ji (1621–1675) – he was the second Sikh martyr.

9 Guru Gobind Singh Ji (1666–1708) – he completed the Guru Granth Sahib Ji and started the community of Sikhs (the Khalsa).

Eventually, all of the teachings of the ten gurus were recorded in the Guru Granth Sahib Ji.

What do Sikhs believe?

The Mool Mantar is the basic statement of belief for Sikhs. It states that there is one God (Il Onkar) and that He has no beginning or end. He is the creator and is all-loving.

Sikhs believe in reincarnation. They believe that when they die the soul lives on and is continually reborn. The aim of life is to break free from being reborn and to be united with God.

Sikhs wear five objects, called the Five Ks, which demonstrate their beliefs. Each object begins with the letter 'K' in Punjabi:

1 **Kachera** – shorts, originally these represented freedom to move when in battle defending the faith.

2 **Kara** – a steel bracelet, symbolic of the fact that God has no beginning or end.

3 **Kesh** – uncut hair. Hair is a gift from God; it is left uncut to show devotion to Him.

4 **Kirpan** – a short sword, symbolic of a Sikh's duty to defend his or her faith.

5 **Kangha** – a wooden comb, used by Sikhs to keep their hair in good condition.

Sikhs believe that all religions are pathways to the one God. They reject the belief that it is right to worship idols (false gods).

Sikhism in the twentieth century

Sikhism originally started in the Punjab in India. Today many Sikhs live in Britain and all over the world. Many people from India, including Sikhs, came to Britain in the 1950s at the invitation of the British government to work due to a labour shortage and the need to rebuild the industry after the Second World War.

Another factor that influenced the movement of Sikhs to Britain was the events of 1947. Up until then India had been part of the British Empire, but in 1947 India became independent and was split into two countries, Pakistan and India. The Sikh home of the Punjab was split right down the middle. Many Sikhs were unhappy with this decision and it resulted in some of them leaving the Punjab. Despite the distance most Sikhs still regard Amritsar as their spiritual home.

Index

Themes in RE:
Learning from Religions

The stimulating issues-based course that raises students' performance

This series for Key Stage 3 explores the major religions through contemporary and relevant themes. Specifically designed to challenge your students' understanding in RE, it provides an ideal grounding for issues-based studies at Key Stage 4.

- The three Student Books, suitable for each year of the Key Stage, create a natural progression of your students' skills through recurring themes.
- The accompanying Teacher's Resource Files contain photocopiable sheets, suggestions for homework and help on assessment and evaluation, so you can accurately monitor your students' progress.
- The series examines six themes across the major world faiths, encouraging your students to learn *both* about and *from* religions.

Themes in RE: Learning from Religions

Student Book 1 0 435 30750 9	**Teacher's Resource File 1** 0 435 30752 5
Student Book 2 0 435 30766 5	**Teacher's Resource File 2** 0 435 30768 1
Student Book 3 0 435 30786 X	**Teacher's Resource File 3** 0 435 30788 6

Heinemann

tel **01865 888068** fax **01865 314029** email **orders@heinemann.co.uk** web **www.heinemann.co.uk**